INSPIRING BASEBALL STORIES FOR YOUNG READERS AND YOUNG AT HEART

LEARN LIFE LESSONS FROM TODAY'S HEROES AND UNDERDOGS TO MOTIVATE KIDS, DEVELOP PERSEVERANCE, MENTAL TOUGHNESS AND TEAMWORK

SUNSHINE CARLSON

CONTENTS

INTRODUCTION

Did you know that the longest baseball game ever played lasted for eight hours? That's right—eight whole hours, as long as a full night's sleep!

One spring evening in Rhode Island, two teams—the Pawtucket Red Sox and the Rochester Red Wings—began a match that would go down in history. In baseball, a game is usually divided into nine segments called innings. In each inning, both teams get a chance to bat and try to score runs while the other team plays defense. After nine innings, the team with the most runs wins. The whole thing usually lasts about two to three hours. That chilly evening, every player from each team was excited and prepared to give it their all. What they didn't know was that their physical and mental strength were about to be tested.

By the end of the ninth inning, neither team had managed to pull ahead. When the score is tied after the ninth inning, the game goes into extra innings... and that's exactly what happened! As the game progressed, the innings kept piling up, with neither team able to break the deadlock. The clock ticked, and fans in the stands, as well as the players on the field, began to realize this wasn't going to be an ordinary game.

What's amazing is that both teams showed off elite skills and seemingly boundless energy. Players were hitting, pitching, catching, and running like there was no tomorrow, even as the night grew darker and colder. The clock struck midnight, but the game kept going. Can you imagine playing baseball when most people are asleep? That's how committed these players were.

By 3 a.m., everyone was utterly exhausted. Some fans had nodded off in the stands, while others had already left, no longer able to keep their eyes open. The players, however, pressed on, fueled by sheer willpower and their desire to win. Then, at 4 a.m., after 32 grueling innings and no sign of the game ending, officials suspended the match to allow the athletes and fans alike to rest. Two months later, the two teams came back, ready to finish what they started. This time, it didn't take long to wrap up the match. In the 33rd inning, the Pawtucket Red Sox scored the winning run. In total, the game lasted a jaw-dropping 8 hours and 25 minutes!

The players who took part in that epic showdown displayed incredible perseverance and mental strength. Despite fatigue and uncertainty, they never gave up. This historic game teaches us an important lesson: No matter how tough things get and no matter how tired you feel, you can achieve great things as long as you keep going.

If you're not feeling like the players in the story right now, if you often find yourself giving up easily or hesitating to even start, fear not! Just like baseball, skills like hard work, teamwork, perseverance, and resilience can all be learned. Even if you don't play baseball, you can still be like the heroes of the story—strong, determined, and ready to tackle any challenge that comes your way.

To help you achieve all of that, this book is here to be your trusty companion! Within its pages, you'll discover a special framework designed to help you become your very best self. It's called GLOVETALES, and here's what it stands for:

- **G**rasp greatness regardless of your size
- **L**earn and practice to get better every day
- **O**vercome obstacles by working together
- **V**alue the people who believe in you
- **E**mbrace the idea of never giving up
- **T**ackle tough times with limitless determination
- **A**lways find a way to bounce back from setbacks
- **L**ead by showing up everyday
- **E**ndure challenges by believing in yourself
- **S**tay strong and keep going, no matter what

We'll dive into each step by exploring the lives of modern-day baseball heroes. These players aren't just winners on the field; they're champions in life too! As you get to know them through their inspiring stories, you'll see how each principle comes to life.

But that's not all! Each chapter is also filled with exciting activities so you can put your newfound knowledge into action. These interactive exercises are crafted to help you think and act like a pro.

So, are you ready to step up to the plate? I hope you are, because you're about to learn what it takes to knock your goals out of the park and hit a home run with GLOVETALES!

GRASP GREATNESS REGARDLESS OF YOUR SIZE

GET TO KNOW YOUR BASEBALL HERO: JOSÉ ALTUVE

"Baseball is the only sport where size doesn't matter, but how big you play."

— JOSE ALTUVE

D o you ever feel small, both inside and out? Maybe these emotions creep in when you look at your classmates who are taller, stronger, or faster than you. Or maybe it's when you're faced with challenges that seem too big to handle, like struggling with a new subject at school or not making the team.

It's normal to feel this way from time to time. Everyone does —even your mom, dad, teacher, or coach. But guess what? Feeling small doesn't mean you can't achieve great things!

Don't believe me? Well, let me tell you a story about someone who had to work extra hard to prove his skills because of his size. His name is José Altuve, and despite his nickname "Gigante," the Spanish word for "giant," he's not particularly big or tall. In fact, he stands as one of the shortest players in the history of professional baseball, consistently shorter than most of his teammates and opponents.

But did he let his size stop him? Absolutely not! Instead, he used it to become one of the greatest. Now, let's learn more about how the little giant José Altuve became such a big name in baseball.

GET TO KNOW YOUR BASEBALL HERO: JOSÉ ALTUVE

José Carlos Altuve was born on May 6, 1990, in Maracay, Aragua, Venezuela, a place known for its deep love of baseball. His father, Carlos, was an avid fan of the sport. In fact, Carlos was watching a baseball match at a stadium when he got the news that his wife, Laste, was at a hospital nearby, ready to give birth to little José.

Carlos' passion for baseball rubbed off on his son. Growing up, José spent much of his time on a dusty field, practicing with his dad, both dreaming that José would someday play in the Major Leagues—the highest level of professional baseball in the United States, where the best players from around the world compete. Despite being a small kid, Carlos always told his son, "You've got to hit to make the Major

Leagues," and José kept that in mind every time he stepped up to bat (para. 13).

José's love for the game only grew stronger as he got older, and his regular practice sessions with his dad started to pay off. At just 16 years old, while José was playing second base for the Venezuelan 16-and-under national team, he caught the attention of scouts from the Houston Astros, a Major League baseball team from Texas.

At first, José's size made the scouts doubt his ability. They even referred to him as "the little guy." However, his skills on the field were undeniable. He impressed the scouts with his speed, agility, determination, and ability to hit the ball consistently. They invited José to officially try out for the team. Sadly, he didn't make the cut, and he came home feeling dejected.

"It was tough. I was 5 feet 5 inches and 140 pounds, so everybody used to say the same thing to me: 'Hey, Jose. You can play. You can hit. But you're not going to make it because you're just too small. Sorry,'" José recalled (Kyle, 2021, para. 25).

Fortunately, the rejection only pushed José to try harder. He was relentless and vowed to never give up on himself. Determined to convince the scouts that he was worthy of joining the Major Leagues, he returned to the tryouts over and over and over again. Finally, the Houston Astros recognized his talent and offered him a contract, turning his and his father's dream of reaching the big leagues into a reality (Pleskoff, 2023).

And the rest, as they say, is history. José turned out to be a sensation in the Major Leagues! He quickly became one of the most exciting players to watch, earning accolades and admiration from baseball fans worldwide.

Tough Times, Big Wins: How José Altuve Beat the Odds!

That being said, even after making it to the pros, Gigante faced some big obstacles. When José joined the Astros, they were in a tough spot with lots of losses.

"I still remember when we lost 100 games three years in a row," José said. "It felt like we were at the very bottom."

The odds weren't in José's favor, as it's extremely rare for players his size to leave a mark on professional baseball. History shows that players who are shorter than five foot six inches usually don't get to play much on the field. Some even only got to bat once in their whole career! If José wanted to prove himself, he had to seize this moment to showcase his skills, even though the team was on a losing streak.

So, instead of giving up, José worked even harder. He showed up at practice everyday, reminding himself to "believe in the process." He changed the way he ate, choosing healthier foods and eating less junk food. During the off-season, instead of going home to Venezuela to rest and spend time with his loved ones, he joined a special training program focused on increasing his strength and agility. He spent hours in the gym, making his body stronger and faster, and in the batting cages, doing drill after drill. José also took this time to learn and listen to advice. He worked with the team's hitting coach to get better at recognizing pitches and understanding the strike zone while also adding a leg kick to his swing for better timing (O'Connell, 2020).

José's resilience and self-belief inspired the entire team. Everyone started to push each other to practice harder and become better. Months later, on a spring day, José looked around at his teammates in the locker room, and it dawned on him: They were going to win.

And he was right! In 2017, the Astros completely turned things around and became the World Series champs. This was the Astros' first-ever championship win, and José completely stood out during the games. Plus, his efforts to boost his team's morale didn't go unnoticed. After the Astros were handed the trophy, José was awarded the American League Most Valuable Player Award (Waldstein, 2019).

José's story goes to show that sometimes what makes you different can become your greatest advantage. His size, which was seen as a weakness by many, actually turned out to be his secret weapon! Now, he views his height not as a disadvantage for himself but for opposing pitchers. Being smaller than most players makes him difficult to target and strike out. Plus, his size allowed him to run faster and move quicker on the field. Most importantly, his perceived disadvantage drove him to work harder and persevere in the face of obstacles.

Achievement Unlocked: Check Out José Altuve's Cool Career Awards!

Eventually, José Altuve's name became synonymous with resilience and tenacity, earning him a reputation as one of the smallest players with the biggest talent. In José's own words, "I'm the same size as everybody else when I'm on the field" (Crasnick, 2012, para. 10). Because of this mindset, he earned a number of cool awards and recognitions, including:

- **Hits Leader (2014–2017):** José led the American League with at least 200 hits per season, showcasing his incredible ability at hitting the ball!
- **Hank Aaron Award (2017):** José was honored with this award for being the best overall offensive performer in the American League that year.
- **Sports Illustrated Co-Sportsperson of the Year (2017):** José was recognized for his contributions both on and off the field, including leadership and community impact.
- **American League Championship Series Most Valuable Player Award (2019):** José was named MVP again as he led his team to another victory with his performance during the 2019 season.
- **All-MLB Team:** The All-MLB Team honors the top players in Major League Baseball for their outstanding performance over the course of the season. José's inclusion in the All-MLB Team in 2019 and 2022 highlighted his consistent excellence and impact on the sport.

- **Silver Slugger Awards:** This award is given to the best offensive players at each position in both the American League and National League. José has won this award five times!
- **Rawlings Gold Glove Award:** José wasn't just good at offense; he was great at defense too, and he has this award to prove it.

These are just some of the many recognitions José received, but there are lots more! For instance, he also broke records when he became the first player to achieve more than 130 hits and 40 stolen bases before the All-Star Game in 2014. Why is that a big deal, you ask? Well, the All-Star Game happens roughly halfway through the Major League Baseball season, meaning José reached these numbers in a relatively short period of time (Hispanic Heritage Month, n.d.).

Additionally, José played for the Venezuelan team at the 2017 World Baseball Classic (WBC), an international baseball tournament where teams from all over the world compete. Think of it as The Olympics of baseball—yep, it's a huge deal! However, this experience was more than just another career milestone for José; it was also a personal one because it allowed him to represent his home country on a global stage. His performance in the WBC solidified his reputation as a world-class player. Most importantly, it inspired many young fans in Venezuela and around the globe. When asked how he felt about being a role model to so many players, José shared that he was extremely honored!

Small Stature, Giant Heart

José Altuve isn't just an icon on the baseball field; he is also dedicated to making a positive impact off the field. This Little Giant has a heart that's larger than life! For instance, when Hurricane Harvey hit in 2017, José teamed up with an awesome 13-year-old kid named Lily DuBose and her charity, Lily's Toy Box. Together, they brought smiles to children affected by the hurricane by giving them toys to replace the ones they might have lost. José didn't just write a check to Lily—he rolled up his sleeves and delivered toys to kids in places like Venezuela too.

José is also a big supporter of Kids' Meals Inc. Ever heard of it? It's an organization whose goal is to make sure no child goes hungry. To this day, José helps provide healthy meals to lots of children in Houston who don't always have enough to eat. He even delivers them himself when he's not practicing!

Additionally, José is an avid supporter of The Sunshine Kids, a group that brings joy to kids with cancer. He is right there in the mix, organizing fun events and raising money to help out. He's all about putting smiles on kids' faces and making sure they know they're not alone and that many people like him care.

And, of course, he's extremely dedicated to supporting the new generation of athletes. When José was a kid, he didn't have the means to buy a brand-new baseball for himself. He had to look for stray balls around the local park, and sometimes, he'd only find one to practice with, which he had to chase after every time he hit it. That's why José knows first-hand how tough it can be to afford stuff like gloves and bats, especially when your family doesn't have much money. When he got his first baseball glove, it meant the world to him, and he promised to someday pay it forward. So, José teamed up with another cool player, David Peralta from the Arizona Diamondbacks, and they collected baseball equipment and gear to send back to kids in Venezuela! They also held a baseball camp and coached 100 young players.

In addition to kids, José also has a soft spot for veterans. Veterans are what we call people who have served in the military, protecting the country and keeping us safe. José is part of this amazing group called K9s for Warriors. What they do is pair up service dogs with veterans who need a little extra help. Service dogs are specially trained to help people do all sorts of things. For example, they can help someone who has trouble seeing by guiding them around safely. Or they can alert someone who has trouble hearing when important sounds, like a doorbell or a phone ringing, happen. Aren't they neat? José thinks so, too! That's why he is super passionate about sharing how awesome these K9s are and how they can make a big difference in veterans' lives (RevUp Sports, 2023).

"Now I am able to help people, it feels really good," José once said (Magruder, 2018, para. 5).

So, even though José is most popular for his killer moves on the baseball field, he's actually also a real-life legend who's passionate about helping others. His big heart proves that regardless of your size, you can make a huge impact in your community.

Did You Know?

Think you know everything about your favorite player, José Altuve? Here is some cool trivia to add to your list of fun facts:

- **José was once sent home from a tryout because people thought he was lying about his age:** When José first tried out for the Astros, the scouts and team staff didn't believe he was old enough to join because of his size! They even told him not to come back, even though he kept insisting he was the right age. Luckily, they eventually believed him because otherwise, they wouldn't have had their future MVP.
- **José is the proud creator of the "jump swing":** Remember when José was training and even added jumps to his swing? Well, that was something completely unique. He first used this technique in a game against the Texas Rangers in 2014. He was batting against pitcher Roman Mendez, who threw a pitch way above the strike zone, almost near Altuve's head. José knew he had to hit the ball, so what did he do? He jumped and swung at the same time. That's how the jump-swing came to be!

- **José is one of only four players since 1901 to lead his league in both hits and steals in the same season before his 26th birthday:** He did it not just once, but twice, in 2014 and 2015! That puts him in the same league as baseball legends like Rickey Henderson, Snuffy Stirnweiss, and Ty Cobb.

- **When José was a kid, he idolized Omar Vizquel, a fellow Venezuelan who played 24 seasons and won 11 Gold Gloves:** José admired Omar so much that he wanted to be just like him when he grew up. Later on, José's dreams more than came true when Omar became a fan of his too (McTaggart, 2014).

- **José's favorite foods:** José loves digging into a hearty plate of rice and chicken, especially when it's homemade. And when he's in New York, you bet he's munching on some delicious New York pizza (Yancelson, 2015).

Chapter Activity: Dream Star

Now that you've read about how José Altuve overcame challenges to achieve greatness regardless of his size, it's time to be inspired to aim high as he did. In this activity, you'll imagine yourself achieving your dreams by creating your very own dream star! Whether you dream of becoming a baseball legend like José, performing on stage as a musician, exploring outer space as an astronaut, or making a difference in your neighborhood, this is your chance to let your imagination shine.

Whenever you're ready, just follow these simple steps:

1. On a piece of paper, cut out a star shape.
2. Think about what you'd love to do when you grow up. It could be something like becoming a famous scientist, an archeologist who travels the world, or an inventor who creates cool robots.
3. Inside the star, write down your dreams. Decorate your star using colored markers or crayons if you feel like it.
4. Find a spot where you'll see your dream star every day—maybe on your fridge, the back of your bedroom door, or your study desk. This will remind you of the amazing things you're working toward.
5. If you come up with new dreams, just add another star!

Remember, with hard work, dedication, and belief in yourself, anything is possible—just like the little giant José Altuve taught us.

* * *

If you ever face a setback or tough obstacle, how will you rise above it?

LEARN AND PRACTICE TO GET BETTER EVERY DAY

"I'm kind of a realist, I know when I suck."

— MOOKIE BETTS

I s there something you wish you could change or get better at? Maybe it's feeling shy or nervous in social situations, like when you have to speak in front of the class or make new friends at school. Or perhaps you wish to be more artistic, so you can bring your ideas to life through drawing or painting. Whatever it is, don't let it bring you down! What if you could find a way to make it better? That's what Mookie did.

Mookie Betts is a baseball icon who has won multiple World Series titles. He is known as an "all-around player," which means Mookie isn't just great at hitting home runs; he's also fantastic at catching tough fly balls and stealing bases to help his team score. But guess what? He wasn't always this good. He had things he wanted to improve, just like you do.

So, how did Mookie Betts go from being a rookie to one of the best baseball players? Let's get to know him to find out!

GET TO KNOW YOUR BASEBALL HERO: MOOKIE BETTS

Mookie's full name is Markus Lynn Betts, and he was born on October 7, 1992, in Nashville, Tennessee. How he got his nickname "Mookie" is actually a fun story: His mom, Diana, wanted him to have a name that honored her sister, who was called Cookie. Diana also loved watching basketball, especially a player named Mookie Blaylock from the Atlanta Hawks. She thought "Mookie" was a cool name, so she gave it to her son (McCaffrey, 2015b). What's even cooler is that Mookie's initials, MLB, are just like Major League Baseball! Maybe it was a sign of what's to come.

Mookie grew up surrounded by sports. His parents, especially his mom, instilled in him a love of athletics. She pushed him to try a number of games, such as football, pool, and basketball. In fact, his mom taught him how to bowl when he was just three years old.

"I never really thought I was going to be a lawyer or anything," Mookie shared. "That never even crossed my mind. It was always some type of professional athlete" (Schube, 2021, para.16).

By the time he was five, his mom tried to sign him up for Little League baseball. However, baseball wasn't really Mookie's first love. While he was an okay enough player, he admitted that he only played in the summer just to hang out with his friends. He also thought the other kids were definitely a lot better at it than him.

"I didn't have a whole lot of power. I wasn't that fast. I was always one of the smallest kids," he recalled (para. 16).

So, it wasn't that much of a surprise to him when several Little League coaches rejected him. However, he still couldn't help but feel dejected every time he heard them say "no."

When his mom saw him about to quit, she took matters into her own hands. She formed a team for Mookie and the other kids who didn't make the cut, stepping up to coach them herself. Their team was allowed to join the Little Leagues, and... well, unfortunately, they sucked! They only managed to win a couple of games and eventually finished last in the league (Huddleston, 2018). Despite their team's disappointing season, Mookie's love for baseball grew stronger. He also developed a new skill: learning how to learn!

"It was a challenge for me to learn," he said. "Anytime I get some type of challenge, my brain flips and tries to solve the puzzle" (para. 12).

And these early lessons set Mookie up for some amazing things in the future. By the time Mookie was in high school, he had starred on John Overton High's basketball, bowling, and baseball teams. His coach at the time, Mike Morrison, noted that Mookie had a knack for quickly replicating something after seeing it just once, and his hand-eye coordination was the best among all the kids in the area, making him unbeatable even at ping-pong.

Mookie was then scouted by many collegiate baseball programs, and he eventually chose to play college baseball at the University of Tennessee. Surprisingly, while he was getting ready to go off to college, he got an offer to play for the Boston Red Sox—a professional baseball team! He accepted the offer, marking the beginning of his pro baseball career.

That being said, it wasn't overnight superstardom for Mookie, but a slow yet steady rise. He began his professional journey playing for different Minor League teams that were part of the Red Sox family. His natural ability to replicate moves easily became much more difficult at this new level of competition, and he struggled to adjust. Despite his talent, Mookie often found himself doubting his abilities and being extra hard on himself when he made mistakes. Fortunately, he had his friends and family to rely on during these challenging times. He called them day and night for months for support.

Thankfully, Shane Victorino, one of his biggest mentors, was also there. Shane encouraged Mookie to keep going and emphasized that messing up is just part of the process. Taking Shane's advice, Mookie eventually realized that he could actually learn from his mistakes.

"You're going to mess up, and you're going to mess up more than once, and you're going to mess up a bunch of different ways," he shared, "That's the frustrating part" (McCaffrey, 2015, para. 61).

So, Mookie kept going. Learning, messing up, and learning some more. He spent a lot of time practicing and figuring out what he could do or improve upon. The baseball field is divided into different areas, each with its own challenges. Mookie tried playing in different spots between the infield and outfield, showing everyone just how adaptable he was. And what do you know? Mookie proved he could excel no matter where he was on the field!

Then, in 2014, Mookie earned a spot on the Pawtucket Red Sox, which is the top level of the minor leagues. And if the Pawtucket Red Sox rings a bell, well, that's because you already know about them! They were one of the teams involved in the longest baseball game ever played, remember?

Anyhow, while playing for Pawtucket, Mookie didn't just stick to one position. He did all that he could to become a well-rounded player. His hard work and dedication paid off because, after only a month, he received the amazing news he'd been hoping for: A chance to play in the Major Leagues!

Mookie made his Major League debut by joining the Red Sox that summer, and the rest, as they say, is history. He went on to dominate the MLB charts, got picked for the All-Star team, won Gold Glove and Silver Slugger awards, and helped the Red Sox win the World Series championship trophy in 2018!

Tough Times, Big Wins: How Mookie Betts Beat the Odds!

After Mookie's remarkable success, especially in the 2018 season, you might think that he had nothing left to improve. But even champions like him are always learning and growing.

In 2020, Mookie was traded to the Los Angeles Dodgers. Imagine you're playing with a group of friends in a game, and suddenly, you have to join a new group with different players. Well, that's what happened to him.

While trades in sports are common and happen for a number of reasons, it was still a bit tricky at first for Mookie. He had to adapt and learn how to work well with his new teammates. He also had to move his family from Boston to Los Angeles. However, Mookie took it all in stride and with a positive attitude.

"It was actually kind of a blessing in disguise. My family loves it. The weather is beautiful," he shared (Reynoso, 2023, para. 10).

But that wasn't all. That same year, Mookie discovered a new weakness: He had trouble hitting against left-handed pitchers! This problem wasn't just for one game—it lasted throughout the season, affecting 28 games. Even though Mookie usually did well against lefties in the past, this issue was a big challenge for the playoffs, where every hit counted a lot. During one game against the Atlanta Braves, Mookie didn't get any hits at all. This made him worried because he didn't want to disappoint his new team, as well as their fans, who were counting on him to lead the team to victory.

Once again, Mookie didn't give up. Even though he was constantly travelling, as he was competing in a series of baseball games, he knew he had to work even harder. He started his training earlier each day to make the most of his time. Then, Mookie listened to feedback from the team's coach and sought help from Doug Latta, a swing expert. Many players were hesitant to work with Doug because they worried about altering their swings, which they were used to and were already well-known for. But Mookie was different. He was open to learning and trying new things if it meant he could improve.

And so, Doug would pick Mookie up from his hotel every morning and take him to the batting cages. There, they worked for hours, making adjustments to Mookie's swing, such as changing how he moved his hands and adding a new leg kick. Mookie practiced tirelessly, hitting against left-handed pitchers over and over again. Even when he had a sore foot from a previous evening's game, he didn't let that stop him. He showed up the next morning at the batting cages with Doug and trained, determined to make progress.

"Hard work beats talent when talent doesn't work hard," he once said (para. 25).

And guess what? All that effort paid off! Mookie started hitting better against left-handed pitchers, and The Los Angeles Dodgers had an incredible season in 2020. They made it through the playoffs, reached the World Series, and bagged their first championship since 1988!

To this day, the 2020 season is still considered a memorable one for The Dodgers and their fans, and Mookie played a big role in it. In fact, he actually sealed the win with a home run in the final game (Apstein, 2020). The key to his success? Learning to embrace failure.

"The road to success is paved with failures and learning from them," said Mookie (Betts, n.d., para. 23).

Achievement Unlocked: Check Out Mookie Betts' Cool Career Awards!

Mookie Betts' story shows us that by learning from failure and practicing hard, we can overcome any weaknesses and achieve amazing things. Even when he was at the top of his game, Mookie was always honest with himself about what he needed to work on. Honesty and willingness to improve are super important for success. Because of his dedication to continuous improvement, he earned a bunch of awesome awards and recognitions, including:

- **Thomas A. Yawkey Award, Red Sox MVP (2016, 2017, 2018):** Mookie was named the most valuable player for the Red Sox three times, showing how important he is to the team.
- **Fielding Bible Award, Right Fielders (2016, 2017, 2018, 2020, 2022):** A right fielder is a player who stands in the right part of the outfield and is responsible for catching fly balls, running fast to stop balls hit far away, and making strong throws to help prevent the other team from scoring runs.

This award is for the best fielders, proving Mookie's skills in catching and defending.

- **Wilson Defensive Player of the Year Award (2016):** This award was given to Mookie for being the best defensive player in the whole league that year!
- **Heart and Hustle Award, Boston Red Sox, and Overall Winner (2018):** This award is given to a player who shows a lot of heart and effort on the field.
- **All-MLB Team (2019, 2020, 2022, 2023):** Mookie was named one of the best players in all of Major League Baseball multiple times!

These are just some of the many awards Mookie has received, but there are many more. In typical Mookie fashion, he always wants to keep improving and reach new heights. Even though he's already accomplished so much, Mookie still believes the best is yet to come. That's why he's continuously training to achieve his ultimate goal: to become a Hall of Famer!

Mookie knows making the Hall of Fame is hard, but that's just the way he likes it. In his own words: "If it was easy, everyone would be doing it. I try to do the things that are really hard" (Toribio, 2022, paras. 8, 14).

Getting Better and Better on and off the Baseball Field

Mookie Betts continues to strive for improvement on and off the baseball field. Remember how his first sport was bowling? Well, he hasn't given up on that passion just because he's now a baseball champ. He has continued honing his skills, just like he did with baseball. And he's pretty good at knocking down those pins! In fact, he has competed in professional bowling events, including those of the Professional Bowlers Association (PBA), where he has played with some of the best bowlers in the world. Mookie, ever the achiever, has even bowled perfect games, scoring a 300, which is the highest possible score in bowling (Selbe, 2022).

But it's not all about sports for Mookie. He loves giving back to his community and helping others, too. He wants to make a positive difference, especially for young people who might be facing tough challenges. That's why he founded the 5050 Foundation, which is named after his jersey number. He says it represents balance and fairness—two things Mookie deeply cares about. His foundation supports important projects like helping kids achieve their dreams, promoting healthy lifestyles, and improving communities by fixing up schools.

He also established his own charity, Acts Inspired by Mookie (AIM). As its name suggests, AIM helps children do well in school by providing resources like books and scholarships. It also encourages kids to stay active by supporting sports and fitness programs, as well as creating safe and happy communities by organizing fun events and building playgrounds. Mookie did this because he believes that every kid should have a shot at dreaming big and should be inspired to work hard to achieve their goals, just like he was able to (*AIM*, n.d.).

"We want everyone to have the opportunity to be successful," Mookie explained. "Most importantly, we want to be a symbol of hope to those less fortunate and remind others that no dream is too big" (*Mookie and Brianna Betts' 50/50 Foundation Makes Donation*, n.d., para. 10).

Mookie's dedication to giving back and his continuous efforts to learn and improve show that he's always striving to be better every day, both as an athlete and as an overall awesome human being!

Did You Know?

Think you know everything about your favorite player, Mookie Betts? Here is some cool trivia to add to your list of fun facts:

- **Mookie holds the record for the most four-hit, five-RBI games in RedSox history:** This means that Mookie has had the most number of games where he got four hits and drove in five runs than any other player in the history of the Red Sox franchise (Parrales, 2020).
- **Mookie is lightning-fast at solving a Rubik's Cube:** New England Sports Network once timed him as he tackled the puzzle, and he finished it in

just a minute and 52 seconds (McCaffrey, 2015a).
Impressive!

- **Mookie loves watching cartoons:** *SpongeBob SquarePants* has been Mookie's favorite show since high school. He says his favorite character is Squidward (Sandler, 2020b).

- **What's in Mookie's bag might surprise you:** When Mookie travels, his suitcase is full of kitchen tools! It includes a camp stove, utensils, cooking oil, and various ingredients and seasonings. He calls it his "travel kitchen," and it helps ensure he always has something healthy to eat while he's on the road.

- **Mookie's favorite post-game snack is a classic:** After giving it his all on the field, Mookie often refuels with a simple peanut butter and jelly sandwich (Garrity, 2023). Yum!

Chapter Activity: Level up Goals

I'm sure you also have weaknesses you want to overcome, just like Mookie Betts did. There's nothing wrong with knowing there's something to improve. In fact, recognizing what you need to work on is the first step to becoming the best version of yourself. It gives you the chance to level up and become even more awesome!

In this activity, you'll make a plan focused on overcoming those roadblocks so you can turn your dreams into reality. And we'll do that by setting SMART goals!

Follow these steps to understand each part of SMART goals:

- **Specific:** Pick the specific weakness you want to work on. Be clear about what you need to improve. For example, instead of saying, "I want to get better at math," say something like, "I want to practice multiplication tables for 15 minutes every day."
- **Measurable:** Decide how you will measure your progress. Make sure you can track improvements. For instance, if you're working on improving your reading, you can measure your progress by keeping track of how many pages you read each day. You could aim to read one extra page every day or finish a chapter within a certain time frame.
- **Achievable:** Set goals that you can reach with effort and hard work. Challenge yourself, but be realistic. Instead of saying, "I want to be the best artist in the world," say, "I want to practice drawing for 20 minutes every day to get better at sketching."
- **Relevant:** Choose goals that are important to you and will help you improve in areas that matter. If you struggle with playing the guitar, a relevant goal might be, "I want to learn a new song on my guitar every month to improve my skills."
- **Time-bound:** Give yourself a deadline to work toward. For example, if you're working on improving your drawing skills, you could set a goal to complete a detailed drawing of your favorite animal by the end of the month. Having a deadline will keep you motivated to practice regularly.

Here's an example of a SMART goal when you put all of the letters together: Instead of saying, "I want to be better at soccer," say, "I'll practice passing with a friend for 20 minutes every day after school for a whole month to improve my accuracy."

Now that you know all about it grab a pen and paper and jot down your new SMART goals! Stick them somewhere you'll see them every day, like on your bedroom wall or the fridge. Use them and Mookie's story to remind us of our commitment to becoming better everyday at something you love.

Think about something you really enjoy doing, like playing a sport or a subject in school. Are there any parts of it that you find a bit challenging? How can you make those tricky parts easier?

OVERCOME OBSTACLES BY WORKING TOGETHER

"I'd rather be in a good position in the playoffs and holding up a World Series trophy than holding up an MVP trophy."

— AARON JUDGE

Is there something that seems too big to handle on your own? Maybe it's feeling overwhelmed by the amount of work you've taken on for a school project or feeling sad but being afraid to talk about it—something that makes you just want to say, "Somebody help!" Whatever it is, you don't have to face it alone.

Aaron Judge, also known as "All Rise," is a baseball sensation who plays for the New York Yankees. He's famous for his powerful home runs and incredible catches in the outfield. But Aaron didn't become amazing overnight. There were times when he struck out or made mistakes on the field too. To overcome these obstacles, Aaron leaned on the people around him. Let's find out how learning to work together with others played a huge role in his success.

GET TO KNOW YOUR BASEBALL HERO: AARON JUDGE

Aaron Judge was adopted on April 26, 1992, the day after he was born, by teachers Patty and Wayne Judge, who raised him in Linden, California. When he was about 10 or 11 years old, he started to notice that he and his brother John, who was also adopted, didn't look much like their parents. This realization sparked questions in young Aaron's mind. His parents didn't shy away from these questions. Instead, they openly discussed adoption with Aaron and John, explaining that they were chosen to be part of their family. Their parents also made sure their home was always filled with love and encouragement.

"Some kids grow in their mom's stomach; I grew in my mom's heart," Aaron shared (Warren, 2022, para. 10).

In high school, Aaron was already a talented athlete who played multiple sports, including football, basketball, and baseball. But juggling them and schoolwork wasn't easy. Aaron's parents knew he loved playing sports, but they also wanted him to do well in school. So, they came up with a plan to help him manage his time.

Every day after school, there was a dedicated time when Aaron would have to work on his homework. His parents made sure he stayed focused and finished his assignments first before hitting the field or court. Even though Aaron had a lot on his plate, there was also an upside: He never got bored!

"Once it got near the end of football, I'd say, 'I can't wait for basketball season to get here; I'm tired of getting hit every day,'" Aaron explained. "Then once it got to the end of basketball, it was, 'I'm tired of running up and down the court; when does baseball start?'"" (Feinsand, 2024, para. 13).

Being amazing at three sports, colleges all over wanted him to join their teams. Some schools even tried to recruit him for football. But Aaron had his sights set on one thing: baseball! It wasn't an easy choice, especially with so many opportunities knocking at his door. But Aaron knew deep down that baseball was his passion, so he wanted to dedicate all his time and energy to it.

When Aaron was 18 and gearing up for college, he received a scholarship to play baseball at California State University, Fresno. But then, in an unexpected turn of events, something remarkable happened: He was drafted by the Oakland A's to play Major League Baseball—it was like a dream come true! However, amidst the excitement, Aaron didn't forget the invaluable lesson his parents had instilled in him about the importance of education. Despite the opportunity to go pro straight out of high school, he chose to pursue his studies at Fresno State. It wasn't an easy decision, but Aaron knew it was what he really wanted to do.

"It was tempting," Aaron admitted. "I just didn't think I was ready or mature enough mentally or physically to start pro ball" (Masih, 2022, para. 10).

When playing for Fresno State, Aaron was introduced to a unique tradition where players were fined for using boastful language like "I," "me," or "my" during practice. So, despite feeling tempted to boast about his own successes sometimes, Aaron never slipped up and was never fined. This helped Aaron remain humble and focused on being part of a team despite his growing fame and success as a star outfielder. And this proved to be a good thing because this humility and focus on teamwork are what once again caught the attention of professional scouts, including the New York Yankees.

The Yankees admired Aaron's size, swing, and athleticism, but what stood out the most was his ability to handle pressure with grace and humility. They believed that Aaron's character and mindset were well-suited for the intensity that comes with playing in New York City, which is why they offered him a chance to be a part of their team in 2013. He accepted and played for different minor league teams within the Yankees family. Then, in 2016, he made his Major League debut, where, at his very first game, he hit a home run!

Since then, Aaron has become one of the most well-known players in baseball. He made waves by winning the American League Rookie of the Year award in his debut season. He's been selected for the All-Star Game an impressive five times, and he's also no stranger to those MVP awards (Grant, 2024). Still, he never forgot his training and always made the team successful.

"I never want to be that guy that's in the spotlight doing this and that," Aaron explained. "If I can go behind the scenes and do certain things to make the whole team better, then that's always my ultimate goal" (Maciborski, 2019, para. 38).

Tough Times, Big Wins: How Aaron Judge Beat the Odds!

Aaron Judge is great, and everyone knows it. However, even great athletes like him still face setbacks. Some of the hardest times for Aaron were when he got hurt. In 2018, a fast pitch hit him on the wrist, and it broke one of his bones. Then, in 2019, he hurt the muscles on his side and had to miss more games. Both times, he had to stop swinging the bat, rest, and ice his injuries because it hurt too much to play (Kuty, 2018; RotoWire Staff, 2024)

Missing games was tough for Aaron, but thankfully, he knew he could count on his teammates for support. Giancarlo Stanton stepped up as the everyday right fielder. Giancarlo was perfect for the job because he was previously an MVP in that position when he was playing for another team. When Aaron got hurt again during the 2024 season, the Yankees stayed strong thanks to new players like Juan Soto and Alex Verdugo, who balanced out the team's offense.

Aaron also experienced being criticized for the way he played. The start of the 2024 season was especially hard on him. Even though The Yankees started strong, winning 17 of their first 26 games, Aaron was struggling at the bat. He struck out a lot and only hit 4 home runs, which was impressive but less than what everyone expected from him. He was even named one of the "10 biggest disappointments of the young MLB season." Ouch!

One specific day was especially rough. On April 20, at Yankee Stadium, Aaron tried to hit the ball four times and missed all four. The crowd booed him! What did Aaron do? As always, he tried not to let it get to him. Aaron's teammates said you could never tell if he's having a great time or a tough time because he always stays cool. He doesn't get too happy when things are going well or too upset when things are tough. He just keeps going, always calm and focused.

"You start off hot, you start off cold, you just can't really look too much into it," Aaron shrugged (para. 15).

Aaron understood that a baseball season offers many opportunities to shine. When his hitting isn't up to par, he shifts his focus to making smart plays, playing solid defense, and contributing in any way possible to help his team win. He's always been aware that a few tough games won't define his overall success.

Fortunately, Aaron's rough patch didn't last long—just about two weeks, actually. Even during that time, he played consistently well, so it was hard to even call it a slump. This quick turnaround is typical of Aaron: Whenever he makes mistakes, he works hard to immediately learn from them. When his hitting wasn't as accurate as he wanted, he turned to Yankees hitting coach James Rowson for help. Aaron even asked his mentors to watch videos of his swing and give him tips on how to improve. Imagine the MVP asking you for advice; that's how dedicated he is to improving!

So, after being booed and called disappointing in April, Aaron was quickly back to being the most exciting hitter in the MLB in May and making headlines with his incredible hot streak.

"I think that's what allows his tougher spells to be shorter because he doesn't get up and down. There's no panic in him," hitting coach James Rowson shared, "He stays the same" (para. 10).

"It's not his first time not playing his ideal. It was just standard procedure. It was only a matter of time until he broke out," teammate Giancarlo added (Thosar, 2024, para. 11).

Achievement Unlocked: Check Out Aaron Judge's Cool Career Awards!

Aaron Judge's story teaches us that in baseball and in life, keeping your cool and working together with others are super important. Aaron trusted his teammates, and they trusted him. They knew that by supporting each other, they could overcome any challenges they faced. Because of this, Aaron earned a bunch of awesome awards and recognitions, including:

- **Home Run Derby Winner (2017):** Aaron was the first rookie in Major League Baseball history to win this exciting competition where players compete to hit the most home runs within a set period.
- **Most Home Runs by a Rookie (2017):** In his first year playing for The Yankees, Aaron hit 52 home runs! That's more than any other rookie in MLB history at the time. He held the record for two years until Pete Alonso of the Mets broke it with 53 home runs in 2019.
- **AL Rookie of the Year (2017):** Aaron was voted the American League Rookie of the Year by a unanimous vote, which means everyone agreed he was the best rookie that year!
- **AL Record for Most Home Runs in a Season (2022):** The same year Aaron was named MVP, he hit an incredible 62 home runs in a single season, breaking a 61-year-old record previously held by Yankees legend Roger Maris.
- **AL Most Valuable Player (2022):** This award is given to the best player in the American League for a whole season, which Aaron won that year.

These are just some of the awesome awards Aaron has won, but there are many more out there. For example, in 2022, he was voted The Associated Press "Male Athlete of the Year." And to top it off, Aaron was also chosen as Time Magazine's "Athlete of the Year."

These honors show just how invaluable Aaron is to his team. His hard work, calm demeanor, and eagerness to learn not only make him a standout on the field but also inspire his teammates to strive for greatness together.

Did You Know?

Think you know everything about your favorite player, Aaron Judge? Here is some cool trivia to add to your list of fun facts:

- **Aaron's nickname "AllRise" comes from the phrase used in courtrooms when a judge enters:** It's an ode to his surname and his powerful presence on the field, both figuratively and literally! You see, Aaron stands at 6 feet 7 inches tall and weighs 282 pounds, which makes him one of the largest and tallest players in MLB.
- **Yankee Stadium has a special section called "The Judge's Chambers" dedicated to Aaron:** It's filled with fans wearing judge's robes and wigs to cheer him on during games!
- **There's a special burger named after Aaron called the "99 Burger":** It's a massive burger with multiple patties, toppings, and a secret sauce. The burger is named after Aaron's jersey number, 99. You'd better grab one quickly because they only make 99 of these burgers for each game! You can get it at the food stand in Section 223 (Kiddle Encyclopedia, 2023).

- **Aaron's guilty pleasure is super delicious:** Aaron is known for loading up on green veggies to stay in top shape. But even this health-conscious slugger's got a soft spot for pizza!
- **Aaron's got a weird superstition involving gum:** Before each game, Aaron pops two pieces of chewing gum into his mouth. If he gets a hit, he keeps chewing them. But if he doesn't, he spits them out and replaces them with fresh pieces. When he's having a great day, the same pieces stay for the whole game (Sandler, 2020a). They probably get a bit tasteless by the end, but it's his unique way of keeping the good vibes rolling!

Chapter Activity: My Team Jersey

The MLB has a super fun event called Players Weekend, which started in 2017. For one weekend in August, players wore cool jerseys inspired by youth league designs. They even got to replace their last names with fun nicknames on the back of their jerseys!

Now, here's another fun fact about Aaron Judge: For the first Players Weekend, he chose to spruce up his jersey by using his nickname, "AllRise," on the back instead of his surname. In 2019, he switched it up again with the nickname "BAJ," which stands for "Big Aaron Judge."

Aaron's creativity with his jerseys shows how important it is to express your team spirit. By choosing fun nicknames and unique designs, he celebrated his connection with his teammates and fans. Now, for this activity, it's your turn to get creative and design your own team jersey!

Just follow these simple steps:

1. Get a blank sheet of paper and some markers, crayons, or colored pencils.
2. Think of a team you are part of or something you love doing with other people. It could be a sports team, a school club, or even a special group name you have with your friends.
3. Choose colors that show what your team is all about. Color your jersey with these special colors.
4. Then, draw a logo or symbol on the front of your jersey. It could be a mascot, a favorite animal, or anything that represents or reminds you of your team. For example, if you and your friends love video games, you could draw an Xbox game controller.
5. If you don't have one yet, think of a fun nickname for yourself and pick a number for your jersey.
6. Add any extra decorations to make your jersey unique. Use stickers, glitter, or anything else you like.

And you're all set! Share your jersey design with your friends, family, or teammates. Explain why you chose the colors, symbols, nickname, and number. Keep your jersey as a reminder of how great it feels to be part of a team and the importance of working together to overcome obstacles.

* * *

Can you think of a time when other people helped you achieve a goal or solve a problem? What are some ways you can support family or friends when they're facing difficulties?

VALUE THE PEOPLE WHO BELIEVE IN YOU

"It's important to surround yourself with people who push you to be better and who believe in your potential."

— CLAYTON KERSHAW

Take a moment to think about all the people who support you every day. Maybe it's your mom who makes you breakfast each morning, your dad who drives you to practice, or your teacher who spends time helping you learn. These people willingly do all of these, often without expecting anything in return. Do you know why? It's because they believe in you! When was the last time you thanked them?

Clayton Kershaw knows that the way you treat the people in your life is a huge part of success. Who is Clayton Kershaw, you might ask? He's the awesome left-handed pitcher of the Los Angeles Dodgers! Let's get to know his story and find out why he cares about the people around him so much.

GET TO KNOW YOUR BASEBALL HERO: CLAYTON KERSHAW

Clayton Kershaw was born on March 19, 1988, in Dallas, Texas. His parents divorced when he was 10, and he was primarily raised by his mom, Marianne. The two lived in Highland Park, where Clayton grew up loving sports. As a child, Clayton always had a baseball nearby and was ready to play at a moment's notice, whether it was in a sandlot or on a local ballfield.

Clayton's mom was his biggest cheerleader back then. Even when money was tight, Marianne worked tirelessly to make sure Clayton never missed a practice or a game. She was always there in the front row, cheering him on and even keeping score on a tiny notepad. With her support and Clayton's natural talent, they made a winning team that set him up for all his big successes (Dedaj, 2023).

But baseball wasn't Clayton's only love as a kid—football was also a blast for him. In fact, he was childhood friends with Matthew Stafford, who would later become a star quarterback in the National Football League (NFL) for the Detroit Lions! Both kids were on Little League baseball teams and later played high school football together.

The two were almost inseparable, having a lot of fun but also pushing each other to improve without realizing it. In fact, it was actually during those times playing with Matthew that Clayton practiced his curveballs. Clayton and Matthew would remain good friends well into their sports superstardom, though they were only dreaming about that future at the time.

In addition to Matthew, Clayton also had an awesome group of school friends who always made him feel supported, even though he was quite a shy kid. Josh Meredith, his childhood best friend, described their group as "not really cool enough to be doing crazy things on Fridays and Saturdays" (para. 13). When the boys weren't playing sports, they were battling it out on Super Smash Bros or looking for a cool pool to dive into. The girls, on the other hand, loved chatting about the latest episode of the Oprah Winfrey show. Everyone attended Bible study and had dinners together at each other's houses. This made such a huge impact on Clayton that he promised that once he got older, his house would always be open for any of his friends to drop by.

"Sunday night dinners are always important," Clayton shared, "and our home will feature a revolving door of people coming and going" (Piellucci, 2023, para. 2).

In high school, Clayton played center in football, but it was baseball where he truly shined. He already had a powerful fastball and a wicked curveball, but between his sophomore and junior years, he experienced a growth spurt. This sudden growth made him even stronger and more dominant on the baseball field!

That being said, Clayton was far from the best. There were dozens of high schoolers in the area who were way better than him. However, this fact didn't discourage Clayton, who always believed in the saying, "Adapt or die." So, he chose to adapt!

The summer before his senior year, he took baseball more seriously and spent countless hours practicing at the batting cages. Then, he met with pitching coach Arthur Ray Johnson, also known simply as "Skip." The only problem was that Clayton and his mom couldn't afford Coach Skip's private lessons. Luckily, Skip believed in Clayton's potential so much that he told them to pay what they could whenever they could. And so Skip drove an hour twice a week, week after week, to coach Clayton basically for free. He recalled Clayton's dad giving him 20 dollars one time, but that was it.

"That's what we do," Skip shared. "That's what we're in coaching for" (McCullough, 2024, para. 26).

Clayton never forgot about Skip's kindness, especially since he learned a lot from these sessions. For instance, Skip had him do a drill called "one-two-three drill." As the name suggests, it involves three steps: raising his hands and right leg together, lowering them together, and then pulling the baseball out of his glove to throw. Even when he was at home, he was required to practice it in front of the mirror. Before, Clayton tended to rush his throws, causing them to veer off course. This drill helped him slow down, making it easier to control the ball and improve his form. It also helped him feel less tired in his arms.

In another drill, Clayton was required to use a hockey puck instead of a baseball to practice his curveball motion. While his curveball was already good, it didn't have much movement. This exercise taught him to put more spin on the ball, making it harder for batters to predict and hit.

Suddenly, Clayton's fastball was blazing past batters at speeds of at least 90 miles per hour—that's like a speeding car on the highway! By the end of his senior year, Clayton had a perfect record of 13 wins and no losses, and he struck out an incredible 139 batters. These amazing stats surprised everyone and caught the attention of Major League scouts.

One of the scouts who noticed how much Clayton had improved was Calvin Jones of the Dodgers. He saw how good Clayton had become, but he and his team hadn't originally come to see Clayton specifically. They were checking out college pitchers in the area, thinking they were more ready for the big leagues than Clayton. Clayton knew he faced tough competition. In fact, six teams would later pass him up. But he was determined to impress the scouts and start earning money through baseball to help his family.

You see, even though Clayton had full scholarship offers from Texas A&M University and Oklahoma State—already a rare feat—he still worried about putting extra financial strain on his mom if he kept going to school. His mom always made sure he had everything he needed and told him not to worry. But Clayton knew she sometimes had to borrow money from others. Baseball gloves and uniforms weren't cheap, after all, and being part of a team was expensive too, with training fees and game costs adding up quickly. Now that he was almost done with high school, he wanted to lighten her load.

"Even with a full scholarship, I didn't know how I was going to be able to go to college," Clayton once shared, "There's stuff that costs money at college" (McCullough, 2024, para. 16)

Fortunately, Clayton didn't have to worry about paying for college after all, as the Dodgers invited him to join their team, kicking off his amazing pro career! With his first paycheck, Clayton did something incredible—he used some of the money to pay off his mom's debts as a big thank you for everything she had done to support his dreams.

"Happiness is not found in material possessions," Clayton once said. "It's found in the simple joys of life and the relationships we cultivate" (Kershaw, n.d., para. 31).

Clayton then spent two years playing in the minor leagues for teams connected to the Dodgers before he got the super exciting call to join the Major Leagues in May 2008, becoming the youngest player in the league at that time!

Since then, Clayton has gone on to achieve amazing feats, such as helping the Dodgers win the World Series and being selected for multiple All-Star Games. He has also earned the nickname "The Claw," partly because it combines parts of his name and partly because he can hold six baseballs in one hand (Adler, 2021; Miller, 2016). Now that's impressive!

Tough Times, Big Wins: How Clayton Kershaw Beat the Odds!

Things were going really great for Clayton. After his Major League debut, he immediately established himself as one of the best pitchers in the league. He received various awards, was named an All-Star many times, and helped the Dodgers win lots of games, including the World Series! Off the field, everything was amazing too. He got married in 2010 and became a dad, something he cherished so much.

"It is the greatest honor of my life to be their father and to have them call me Dad," Clayton once wrote. "Of course, there's no way I could be even half the dad that I am if it weren't for my wife, Ellen, being so incredible" (Kershaw, 2019, paras. 89, 95).

But then, just before Mother's Day in 2023, tragedy struck: Clayton's mom, Marianne, passed away. Losing someone you love is one of the hardest things anyone can go through, and it was especially tough for Clayton, as Marianne had been his biggest supporter since the very beginning. She bought him his first baseball, took him to his first game, and comforted him the first time he ever lost.

The day after Clayton received the devastating news, he and Ellen were supposed to go to the grand opening of a youth baseball field in Inglewood, California, which they helped fix up. Clayton understandably couldn't make it; Ellen went instead and told everyone why Clayton wasn't there. In her speech, she dedicated the field to Marianne to honor her memory (Neumann, 2023).

Clayton and his family received an outpouring of support from friends and baseball fans. Clayton really valued the people in his life, and that's why, during the toughest moments, their support meant so much to him. Three days later, he expressed a heartfelt message: "It's been humbling to see how many people reached out, and I'm thankful for that. Just thank you to everybody that's reached out" (Villas, 2023, para. 3).

This difficult moment in Clayton's life teaches us that when we cherish and support those in our lives, they, in turn, support us through tough times. Being there for each other makes us stronger and helps us get through any challenges together.

Achievement Unlocked: Check Out Clayton Kershaw's Cool Career Awards!

Thanks to his hard work and the support of many people who believed in him, Clayton is the amazing athlete he is today and has received a number of awards and recognitions, including:

- **Cy Young Award (2011, 2013, 2014):** This award is given to the best pitcher in each league based on their performance throughout the season. Clayton won this award three times by the age of 26, which is a record! Most players who receive this award achieve it only once or twice.

- **NL MVP Award (2014):** This award is given to the player who is the most important to their team's success, and Clayton was named MVP in 2014, making him the first pitcher to win this award since 1968, alongside baseball legend Bob Gibson (Harrigan, 2020).
- **MLB All-Star (2011–2017, 2019, 2022):** Being selected as an All-Star means Clayton was considered one of the best players in the league. Clayton has been named an All-Star nearly every year since 2011.
- **World Series Champion (2020):** Clayton helped lead the Los Angeles Dodgers to win the World Series in 2020—their first win since 1988!
- **Branch Rickey Award (2013):** This award is given to a player who makes a significant difference on and off the field by helping their community and being a role model to others. Clayton won this award because he is not only a great pitcher but also a great person who inspires and supports others (*Clayton Kershaw Awards*, n.d.).

These are just a few of Clayton's many accomplishments; there are lots more out there. Besides winning awards, he also gives back to his community in meaningful ways. In 2011, he and Ellen started something amazing called Kershaw's Challenge.

It all began when they met a young girl named Hope in Zambia. Hope had faced tough times, like being sick and homeless. Clayton and Ellen decided to help by making sure she had what she needed, like food and supplies. But they realized that Hope also needed a safe house and loving parents. So, they started Kershaw's Challenge to help kids like Hope find a family. Kershaw's Challenge has improved the lives of many children all over the world, from Los Angeles to the Dominican Republic (Kershaw's Challenge, n.d.).

Clayton knows how important it is to have people who believe in you, just like his mom, Skip, his group of friends, his teammates, and all the fans who believe in him. That's why Clayton now pays it forward.

"Baseball is great. I love it. I'm thankful I get to play it," Clayton explained, "But at the same time, I know it's a platform to be able to do other things" (Chu, 2023).

Did You Know?

Think you know everything about your favorite player, Clayton Kershaw? Here are some cool trivia to add to your list of fun facts:

- **Clayton Kershaw is the strikeout king of the Dodgers:** When he made his 2,697th career strikeout, he beat the record held by Hall of Famer Don Sutton since 1979 (Ardaya, 2022). Now, Clayton holds the top spot for the most strikeouts in Dodgers history!

- **Clayton's game-day routine involves a hearty bowl of cereal:** According to his wife, every day begins with Clayton mixing his favorite Golden Grahams with another cereal. It's his go-to meal, no matter where he's playing!

- **Clayton's jersey number is a nod to his favorite player, Will Clark:** Despite Will Clark playing for the rival team, the Giants, he also played for the Texas Rangers while Clayton was growing up. That's why Clayton has been a huge fan ever since (Sandler, 2021).

- **Clayton is not just a powerful pitcher; he's also a record-breaking hitter:** He holds multiple records for home runs hit by a pitcher, and get this: he's even hit a grand slam! That makes him one of the coolest pitchers ever when it comes to batting.

- **Clayton's connection to space is out of this world:** He's actually the great-nephew of Clyde Tombaugh, the astronomer who discovered Pluto! Clayton has even shared that his family felt really bummed when Pluto got downgraded from being a planet to a dwarf planet (Mustard, 2015).

Chapter Activity: Thank You Card

Just like Clayton Kershaw, you have people in your life who support and cheer for you too. It's important to recognize and value these special people. So, for this activity, you'll create a thank you card to show your appreciation. It's a simple and fun way to say, "Thank you!"

Ready to brighten someone's day? Just follow these steps:

1. Think about someone who has supported you, like your parents, a teacher, or your best friend. This could be anyone who has helped you, encouraged you, or made you feel cared for.
2. Take a piece of paper and fold it in half to make a card.
3. On the front of the card, write "Thank You" in big, colorful letters.
4. Inside the card, write a message to the person you are thanking. Here's a simple way to do it:

- Start with "Dear [Name],"
- Write why you are thankful for them. For example, "Thank you for always helping me with my homework" or "Thank you for being a great friend."
- End with a nice closing, like "Sincerely," "Love," or "Your friend," and then sign your name.

1. If you want, you can add drawings, stickers, or decorations to make the card extra special!
2. Hand your card to the person you made it for, or ask an adult to help you mail it if they live far away.

Remember, a simple thank you can show someone how much you appreciate their support. It's like giving a little gift of happiness! Try to say thank you often to the special people in your life.

* * *

Think about a time when someone's belief in you made a difference. How did it affect your actions and attitude?

EMBRACE THE IDEA OF NEVER GIVING UP

"Success is not about winning, it's about giving it your all every time."

— CODY BELLINGER

Are you thinking about giving up on something important or fascinating to you right now? Whether it's a new sport, a demanding school project, or a beloved hobby, it's natural to feel like throwing in the towel when things get tough. But imagine how great it would be when you finally succeed! The trick is to keep trying, just one more time. Remember, even the best athletes, musicians, and scientists had to push through some tough times before achieving their dreams.

Take Cody Bellinger, for example. He had to overcome many obstacles, and now he's a World Series champ, All-Star, and MVP! What adversities did he overcome before achieving this level of success? Let's get to know more about him to find out.

GET TO KNOW YOUR BASEBALL HERO: CODY BELLINGER

Cody Bellinger was born on July 13, 1995, in Scottsdale, Arizona. Sports were a big part of his childhood. His mom, Jennifer, was a star volleyball player in college. Meanwhile, his dad, Clay, played Major League Baseball, winning two World Series championships with the New York Yankees. Needless to say, with a two-time World Series champ for a dad, Cody was exposed to baseball early on. He played in Little League and often spent time in Major League clubhouses.

When Cody was just 10 years old, he got to live every young baseball player's dream: playing in the Little League World Series! It's like the Major League World Series but for kid athletes. So yeah, it's a pretty big deal. Cody's team from Chandler, Arizona, faced teams from all around the world. Despite being one of the smallest and youngest kids there, Cody's skills really wowed the crowd when he hit a home run in one of the games (Trezza, 2017). Then, he successfully hit the ball three times in a row!

Playing in the Little League World Series was a huge moment for Cody because, even though his team didn't win, it made him realize just how much he truly loved baseball.

"It was fun," Cody beamed (Harris, 2019, para. 16).

Fast forward to high school. Despite his Little League World Series experience, Cody didn't immediately qualify for Hamilton High's varsity team. Instead, he spent two years on junior varsity (JV). Being placed on JV means you're good but not quite at the highest competitive level yet. Also, Cody was considered thin and not exactly the right size for a baseball player. Even after growing to six feet tall, he was still described as more skinny than strong.

"He was kind of like a beanpole," recalled Farhan Zaidi, the former general manager of the Los Angeles Dodgers, when asked about his first impression of Cody (McCullough, 2017, para. 19).

Rather than feeling discouraged, Cody used this feedback as an opportunity for growth. If he wasn't quite good enough for varsity yet, then he would absorb all the knowledge that he could from his JV coach and teammates to improve. If he wasn't considered a strong hitter yet because of his physique, then he would focus on improving his batting along with other skills that could benefit the team.

So, off Cody went, not only perfecting his swing but also mastering pitching and exploring other field positions. Because of his dedication, Cody achieved an amazing feat: pitching a four-hit, complete-game shutout in a national tournament! That means he allowed the opposing team only four hits throughout the entire game and prevented any runs from scoring.

Looking back, Cody feels grateful that he didn't let setbacks stop him. In fact, he now has some great advice for kids who might be in the same situation: "If you're a smaller guy on the field, just keep going. Work on the small things so that when you get older and bigger, you can catch up to those guys who've always been bigger than you" (Hall, 2018, para. 4).

During his senior year, Cody stood out even more. He was recognized as one of the top players in the country, earning the prestigious 2013 Rawlings-Perfect Game 2nd Team All-American award! This honor is reserved for high school athletes who demonstrate exceptional skill, dedication, and performance.

Additionally, Cody received a full scholarship offer from the University of Oregon. But,Cody's college plans took a different turn when the Los Angeles Dodgers asked him to join their team straight out of high school. He decided to accept it, and that's how Cody's professional career began in 2013.

He then went on to play in the Minor Leagues for a few years before making his Major League debut in 2017 (*Cody Bellinger Biography*, 2020). A few years later, he was named MVP, racked up tons of awards, and set and broke records left and right. He even snagged the coveted World Series Championship ring!

"Stay committed to the process, and the results will come," Cody once said (Bellinger, n.d., para. 40).

Tough Times, Big Wins: How Cody Bellinger Beat the Odds!

After Cody made his Major League debut, he hit the ground running! He immediately became a star player for the Dodgers and gained a reputation as one of the best young power hitters. In 2019, at just 23 years old, Cody hit an amazing 47 home runs and was named the National League MVP, surpassing more experienced players. He also made history by becoming the first rookie ever to hit 10 home runs in a span of 10 games (Nathan, 2017).

In 2020, during a big game against the Atlanta Braves, Cody hit an epic home run that put the Dodgers ahead and closer to the World Series. He was so excited that he celebrated by giving his teammates big chest bumps and high-fives. But, when he bumped arms with Kiké Hernández, Cody's right shoulder popped out of place. Ouch!

He had to rush to the locker room, where paramedics quickly put his shoulder back in place. Everyone thought he'd be out for the game, maybe even the rest of the season, but Cody came back out like a champ and kept playing. He even helped his team win!

You might think the injury would have dampened his spirits, but Cody actually turned the whole experience into something positive. To prevent it from happening again, he started tapping toes with his teammates whenever he hit a home run. Fans enjoyed this new celebration style as much as the players did.

"I said if I ever hit one, I'm not touching anybody's arm. I'm going straight foot," Cody shared when asked about the new home run celebration trend he created. "It was pretty funny" (Monagan, 2020).

Soon enough, Cody found himself in the World Series again, but now as a Major League pro. And this time, he didn't come home defeated! The Dodgers were crowned champions—the team's first since 1988 and a first for Cody himself. From his days in Little League to this, Cody has truly come a long way.

Just think, if Cody had given up at age 11 after losing in the Little League World Series, or in high school when he only qualified for the JV team, or even after he hurt his shoulder, he never would have become a World Series champ.

"I'll tell them what resilience is, how our backs were against the wall and it made us stronger," Cody said in an interview after the win (Alipour, 2020, para. 19).

Unfortunately, the celebrations didn't last long. Just a month after their big win, Cody had to undergo surgery for his shoulder. And then more injuries came his way. Over the next three years, Cody dealt with a fractured shin, a broken rib, a knee injury, and a strained left leg muscle. Despite Cody's determination to shrug off each one, they all added up and undeniably took a huge toll on his body and performance.

His once-unbeatable power and precision, which had made him a fan favorite, began to fade. He couldn't swing the bat as forcefully or accurately as before, causing his batting average to drop drastically. But, of course, this is Belli—he wasn't just going to give up! Instead, he committed himself to rigorous training sessions, spending hours working out at the gym. His focus was on strengthening his core and lower body in the hopes of stabilizing his swing.

Cody also teamed up with the team's coaches, tirelessly adjusting his stance and experimenting with new strategies during each game. Sometimes, a tweak would show promise, and he'd start hitting better for a brief period of time. But the ups and downs were tough, especially with fans and critics weighing in. By 2021, Cody ranked among the lowest MLB hitters (Harris, 2023). His decline was described as a rapid rise followed by a steep fall unlike anyone's ever seen before. As his stats continued to plummet, fans grew increasingly disappointed, and Cody felt the pressure mounting.

Then came another blow: Despite being a former MVP, the Dodgers made the difficult decision to part ways with him. This meant he had to leave the team he had grown up with. It was hard for Cody because he had once thought he'd be a Dodger forever. Still, he tried to keep an open mind.

"Life is not always planned," Cody said. "I just try to be in the moment and appreciate what comes next for me" (Pasillas, 2023, para. 4).

And what came next was a new team and a new city: the Cubs in Chicago. While packing up his life in LA was undoubtedly difficult, Cody wasted no time getting to work, excited to make a good first impression in his new Cubs jersey. He spent hours in the batting cages with his dad, and once he settled in with the Cubs, he teamed up with coaches who he had worked with before and knew well. Together, they fine-tuned his stance and adjusted his swing, focusing on every detail—from reading pitches to keeping his hips steady and tweaking his grip on the bat.

It wasn't just about physical adjustments, though; after all the setbacks, Cody needed to believe in himself again. Cubs coaches tremendously helped him in this process. They encouraged him to tune into his body, trust his instincts more, and ease off on the technicalities. Most importantly, they reminded him just how awesome he was (Rogers, 2023). With their support, Cody persevered, determined to show he still had it in him. Every swing, every practice session—it was all about reclaiming his place at the top!

And reclaim his place, he did. With his confidence back on track and his body stronger than ever, Cody made an incredible comeback! In just his first season with the Cubs, he hit an impressive 26 home runs, knocked 29 doubles, and brought in 97 runs for the team. Cody was also making contact with the ball like never before, with an 81.2% success rate. He even hit his 17th career multi-homer game and became the seventh player in Cubs history to have at least 20 homers and 20 steals in a single season.

But it didn't stop there; Cody was also one of only four MLB players in 2023 to hit at least .300 with 25-plus homers and 20-plus stolen bases, joining elite players like Ronald Acuña Jr., Shohei Ohtani and Freddie Freeman. His amazing performance earned him a Silver Slugger!

Fellow athletes were also so impressed by Cody that he was voted as the National League's Comeback Player of the Year. Cincinnati Reds catcher Luke Maile and fellow Cubs teammate Dansby Swanson were two of those who cheered him on.

"It's just cool to see a guy overcome all of that, especially the way he's done it," Luke said.

"Talent just doesn't leave you. Confidence is a real thing. You get that belief back in yourself, and things can take off," Dansby added.

As for Cody, he's just glad he kept trying.

"I'm having fun again," he beamed (Nightengale, 2023, paras. 27, 34, 44).

Achievement Unlocked: Check Out Cody Bellinger's Cool Career Awards!

Cody Bellinger's story shows that persistence and determination pay off big time! Even when faced with challenges, Cody never gave up and kept pushing himself to the best of his abilities. His determination led to him earning a bunch of awesome awards and recognitions throughout his career, including:

- **National League Rookie of the Year (2017):** Cody won this award the first year he joined the Major Leagues, showing everyone he was a rising star.

- **Youngest Dodgers Player to Hit for the Cycle (2017):** Cody hit a single, double, triple, and home run all in one game! This made him the youngest player in Dodgers history to do so.
- **Fastest Dodgers Player to Reach 100 Career Home Runs (2019):** Cody set this record by hitting 100 home runs faster than any other Dodgers player before him!
- **MLB All-Star (2017, 2019):** Twice selected to the MLB All-Star Game, Cody showcased his talent alongside other top players in the league.
- **Silver Slugger Award (2019):** This award honors Cody as one of the best offensive players in his position, thanks to his outstanding batting skills.

These are just a few of Cody's most impressive achievements; there are many more out there. In fact, he's also known for hitting the most home runs in his rookie season! Plus, he's not just focused on pushing himself; he wants to inspire others to keep going too. One great example is from 2019 when Cody joined the #DontRetireKid campaign. This campaign was all about encouraging young athletes to stick with sports and not give up, even when things get tough.

Cody teamed up with Clayton Kershaw. Do you remember him from the last chapter? They recorded a video reaching out to a nine-year-old baseball player named Colt, who was feeling burnt out and was thinking about quitting.

"The game of baseball, or sports in general, is hard. Just come back stronger and don't retire, kid," was Cody's message to Colt.

When Colt saw the heartfelt messages from Cody and Clayton, he changed his mind and decided to postpone his retirement. Colt even wrote a touching letter back to the two superstars, expressing how their words had made him excited to keep playing baseball again (Green, 2019).

Cody's involvement in the campaign shows just how much he cares about encouraging the next generation, probably because he was a Little Leaguer himself. By sharing his own love for the sport and encouraging kids like Colt, Cody is making a big difference in the lives of young athletes everywhere. Now that's an achievement that's hard to top!

Did You Know?

Think you know everything about your favorite player, Cody Bellinger? Here are some cool trivia to add to your list of fun facts:

- **There's a character inspired by Cody in the video game *Assassin's Creed Valhalla*:** Players must defeat Viking Otta Sluggasson, who swings a tree trunk like a baseball bat. Cody, who loves gaming, used motion capture technology to record his movements, and his own baseball bat served as Sluggasson's weapon (Kiddle Encyclopedia, 2024c). Pretty cool!

- **Cody listens to meditative music on his way to the field:** He says it helps him feel relaxed and ready to play. He also listens to "zenful" music while working out instead of hip hop, rap, or country music (Scipioni, 2021).

- **Cody's breakfast routine is super specific and delicious:** Every morning, he used to head over to iHop for his favorite—banana Nutella crepes with a side of hash browns, bacon, and eggs (Clair, 2018). But, rumor has it that in 2023, his go-to crepe combo was discontinued. Imagine waking up to find out your favorite breakfast is no longer on the menu!

- **Like father, like son:** Cody sported jersey number 35 with the Dodgers from 2017 to 2022—the same number his dad, Clay, proudly wore during his Major League days with the Yankees and Angels (Randhawa, 2024). How sweet!

- **Cody's nicknames:** While most people call him "Belli," he once earned the nickname "CodyLove" during Spring Training in 2016. This was inspired by teammate Joc Pederson's hashtag #JocLove, and it was a playful effort by his team to boost Cody's social media following (Duarte, 2017). And it worked!

Chapter Activity: Keep Going Bookmark

Sometimes, we all need a little reminder to stay motivated and keep pushing forward. In this activity, you'll create a motivational bookmark to inspire yourself to never give up!

It's a fun and creative way to remind yourself that, with perseverance, anything is possible.

Are you ready to create your bookmark? Follow these simple steps:

1. Choose a sturdy piece of colored paper or cardstock for your bookmark base.
2. Take your colored paper or cardstock and cut out a strip about two inches wide and six inches long. This will be the base of your bookmark.
3. On one side of the bookmark, write something to motivate you, like "Keep swinging for the stars!" or "Never give up on your dreams!" Use colorful markers or pencils to make the letters bold and eye-catching.
4. Write your name or initials on the back of the bookmark to make it special and unique to you.
5. Slip your bookmark into your school notebook, favorite book, or sports magazine so that you are always reminded to stay determined.

Just like Cody Bellinger, you have the power to persevere through challenges and never give up on your dreams. Whether it's learning a new skill, tackling a problem, or making new friends, keep pushing forward!

* * *

Can you think of a time when you wanted to quit something? What made you keep going instead?

Step up to the Plate!

"All I know is when we win a game, it's teamwin. When we lose a game, it's a teamloss."

— COACH MORRIS BUTTERMAKER, THE
BAD NEWS BEARS

The reason GLOVETALES works so neatly is that baseball is such a great metaphor for life. There are wins and there are losses, but no matter what, you just have to keep showing up and being there for your team. Each day is a new game, and as each of our baseball heroes shows us, no matter what happened in the last game, you have to put your losses behind you, step up to the plate, and give it your all.

No baseball player ever works alone: It's all about the team. They support, motivate, and learn from each other in order to build the best team they can. This is something we can apply to life too. Humans are social animals, and no matter what our lives are like, they always involve other people— people who support us, motivate us, and share their experiences, which we can then learn from. When we're conscious about this, we can make ourselves even better team players, taking every opportunity we can to support other people and help them achieve their goals—and the great thing about this is that when we do, we give ourselves even more opportunities to learn and grow.

In the spirit of this, I'd like to ask you to step up to the plate and share the GLOVETALES framework of self-improvement with other people so that they, too, can benefit. There are a number of ways you can do this: You can tell your friends about what you've learned here, or you can share this book with them. But by far the easiest thing you can do—and the one that will allow you to hit the ball the furthest—is write a review so that this book and the baseball heroes within it reach even more people.

By leaving a review of this book on Amazon, you'll make it easier for new readers to find it, spreading motivation and inspiration far and wide—just like the best baseball players.

Reviews help new readers to make decisions about the books they want to read, and simply by leaving a few sentences, you can inspire someone else to explore the GLOVETALES framework and set out on an epic journey to become the best version of themselves.

Thank you so much for your support. We're all part of a huge team, and your role is so important.

Scan the QR code below

TACKLE TOUGH TIMES WITH LIMITLESS DETERMINATION

"When you come back on top after you've fallen, it's a better story."

— FREDDIE FREEMAN

Are you going through something really difficult right now? It might feel like things won't get better, but remember, tough times don't stick around forever. You've got the strength inside you to tackle these challenges head-on! In fact, facing these tough moments helps you become even stronger.

Take it from baseball legend Freddie "Frito" Freeman, best known for his sweet left-handed swing and exceptional fielding skills. Freddie hasn't just carved out a remarkable career; he's also known as "the friendliest man in baseball."

But Freddie is no stranger to difficulties and setbacks. Let's find out how he tackled them to become both a successful athlete and an overall awesome person!

GET TO KNOW YOUR BASEBALL HERO: FREDDIE FREEMAN

Freddie Freeman was born on September 12, 1989, in Villa Park, California. His parents were both from Canada, so Freddie was born with dual citizenship. That means that someone is considered a citizen of two countries at the same time, making Freddie both American and Canadian.

Freddie's love for baseball started with his dad, Frederick, who played a big role in making him the successful player he is today. Almost every day when Freddie was growing up, he and his dad would head to a nearby baseball field with a bucket full of exactly 48 balls. For an hour straight, Frederick would pitch to little Freddie.

In the first bucket, Freddie aimed to hit the ball to left field. In the second bucket, he aimed straight down the middle. Finally, in the third bucket, Freddie hit balls all over the field, but they almost always went to left field. Little did they know, this was helping Freddie develop his signature way of hitting, which would be envied by other players decades later. They didn't follow a fancy plan or have a coach, though; they were just doing it for fun.

By the time Freddie was six years old, his talent on the baseball field was off the charts! While playing Tee Ball, he hit the ball so hard that his swing was considered too dangerous for kids his age. Because of this, Freddie had to practice and play with kids who were older than him. When he was seven, he was placed on a team of nine-year-olds. When he turned nine, he was placed with twelve-year-old kids.

On the other hand, Freddie's mom, Rosemary, was his biggest fan. She didn't know much about baseball, but when she saw how much her son loved it, she bought a book called "Baseball for Dummies" to learn all about the sport. She was always there for Freddie and his brothers, cheering them on. She even earned the nickname "Button Mom" in Little League because she always wore buttons with their pictures on them. Overall, Freddie had a happy childhood with a loving family and lots of baseball.

Unfortunately, when Freddie was 10 years old, tragedy struck: His mom passed away from melanoma, a type of skin cancer. It was a very sad and difficult time for Freddie. To help cope with the loss, he and his dad spent even more time playing baseball together. Their practice sessions, which used to last just an hour, now stretch longer. As Freddie hit the ball over and over, he thought of his mom and the happy times they had together, and his love for baseball grew stronger. He also made a promise to be good, believing his mom was always watching over him.

"He felt like, to honor his mom, he had to be a great kid," Freddie's dad shared. "That was it. When he was 10, that's what he decided he was going to be" (Kepner, 2021, para. 3).

Even during his time at El Modena High School, Freddie and his dad continued their daily batting practice sessions. But, since Freddie was a part of the school's varsity team, they often had to stay late after his practices to do their three-bucket routine. His dad also made time during his lunch break as a public accountant to join Freddie at the high school for extra time.

However, his dad wasn't the only one guiding Freddie. He found a new mentor in the form of the team's head coach, Steve Bernard. Coach Bernard made sure that Freddie didn't just know how to hit but also how to pitch. By the time Freddie was a senior, he had played many positions in the field, from first base to third base and pitcher. Most importantly, Coach Bernard was there for Freddie when he missed his mom. They spent hours together on the field, practicing and talking about life.

"There were some moments that were tough for him," Coach Bernard shared once; "the ability to go and play ball allowed him to get through some of those difficult times" (DiGiovanna, 2020).

With the support of his dad and Coach Bernard, Freddie became a standout player. In his final season at the school, he helped his team win the Century League title—their first in 16 years! Afterward, Freddie's name appeared in the papers when he was honored as the 2007 Orange County Player of the Year by the Orange County Register (Osborne, 2022). He left such a mark on the school that they decided to honor him by no longer allowing any other players to wear jersey number 9—Freddie's jersey number!

Professional scouts were really impressed with Freddie's skills, both as a hitter and a pitcher. He had an outstanding batting average, and his fastballs flew as fast as a race car at 96 miles per hour. While Freddie was getting ready to play college baseball for California State University Fullerton, something amazing happened: The Atlanta Braves, one of the big teams in MLB, offered him a spot on their team instead! Freddie said yes, starting his pro baseball career at just 17 years old—the youngest player on the team once again (Pleskoff, 2022).

After accepting the Braves' offer, Freddie spent a few years playing on their Minor League teams. During the start of the 2009 season, Baseball America recognized him as one of the best young players in the Braves' organization. Then, in 2010, when Freddie was 20 years old, he finally received the call to play in the Major Leagues!

He went on to have an amazing debut year, hitting 21 home runs and finishing second in the National League Rookie of the Year award, right after his teammate Craig Kimbrel. Since then, Freddie has soared to the top, being named an All-Star multiple times, winning the MVP award, and even becoming a World Series champion!

There were moments when Freddie felt like giving up. His mom's birthdays were especially hard on him. But he didn't let those tough times stop him. With grit and determination, he kept going, knowing that every challenge was making him stronger and better.

"I'm thankful for every setback and adversity I've faced. They've made me stronger and more determined to succeed," Freddie firmly believed (Freeman, n.d., para. 44).

Tough Times, Big Wins: How Freddie Freeman Beat the Odds!

Freddie used the tough times as fuel to succeed. And because skin cancer took a loved one from him, Freddie has always taken sun protection seriously, especially since he spends a lot of time outdoors. He wore arm sleeves to protect himself from harmful rays, and he encouraged his teammates and fans to do the same. One time, to raise awareness, he and the Atlanta Braves held a special "Freddie Sleeve Day," where fans could buy sleeves designed by him. All the money was donated to cancer research.

However, in 2016, painful memories came rushing back when Freddie received some bad news. There was a suspicious mole on his back—it turned out to be cancer. Thanks to his regular check-ups, they spotted it early. Freddie had surgery to remove it, and afterward, he was fortunately cancer-free. After taking it easy for a bit, he was back on the baseball field in just a matter of days. Even with a few stitches in his back, Freddie maintained a positive attitude.

"If you see blood on my shirt, don't freak out," he joked. "The stitches just came out. That's all" (James, 2016, para. 7).

Freddie once again turned the experience into something good: He partnered with SUBWAY in Atlanta for a fundraising event called "Freddie Freeman's Hugs and Subs" during Childhood Cancer Awareness Month. This campaign allowed customers in North Georgia to make donations to the Child Life Zone at Scottish Rite Hospital. The customers got a personalized "I Hugged Freddie" badge for their generosity (*Freddie Freeman of the Atlanta Braves Fights Back for His Mom*, 2016).

The year after that, Freddie made a surprising decision: He chose to play for Team Canada in the World Baseball Classic. Fans were initially confused. The U.S. team was the favorite, and the Canadian team wasn't even expected to win. So, why was he playing for them? In fact, the Canadian team did lose, but to Freddie, it was one of the coolest experiences in his baseball career because he did it for his mom.

"There's no greater way for me to honor her and my family than to play for her country," Freddie explained. "It's something I'll never forget" (Bowman, 2017, paras. 2, 9).

Achievement Unlocked: Check Out Freddie Freeman's Cool Career Awards!

Even when faced with huge challenges, Freddie never gave up. Instead, he used these tough times to push forward and create something positive. Because of this, Freddie has received a number of awards and recognitions, including:

- **All-Star (2013, 2014, 2018, 2019, 2021–2023):** Freddie has been selected to the All-Star Game numerous times, where only the best players get to compete!
- **National League MVP (2020):** The National League Most Valuable Player award is given to the player who made the most impact on the team based on overall performance and leadership during the season. Freddie earned this prestigious award in 2020!
- **NL Hank Aaron Award (2020):** This award goes to the best offensive player in the National League. Freddie won it in 2020 because he's amazing at scoring runs and helping his team win!
- **World Series champion (2021):** In 2021, Freddie and his team, the Atlanta Braves, won the World Series—a moment every baseball player dreams of!
- **Babe Ruth Award (2021):** The Babe Ruth Award is given to the Most Valuable Player of the postseason. Freddie received this prestigious award in 2021, recognizing his exceptional performance during the playoffs and World Series combined (Kiddle Encyclopedia, 2024d).

These are just some of the awards Freddie has received; there are many more out there. In fact, Freddie's amazing talent and hard work have also led him to break records. For example, in one season, he hit an incredible 53 doubles for the Los Angeles Dodgers. This broke a record that had been set way back in 1929—almost a hundred years ago! These achievements reflect Freddie's dedication, skill, and impact on the game of baseball, making him a role model for aspiring athletes everywhere (Stevens, 2023).

Did You Know?

Think you know everything about your favorite player, Freddie Freeman? Here is some cool trivia to add to your list of fun facts:

- **Freddie is ambidextrous:** That means he's skilled at using both his left and right hands. In fact, he bats left-handed and throws with his right. It's quite a rare ability!
- **Freddie was banned from making a dance move in 2008:** While playing for the single-A Rome Braves in his Minor League years, the team officially banned him from ever doing "the worm" dance move because they were worried he might get hurt (Lord, 2023). His wife, Chelsea, said he was actually really good at it!
- **Freddie is known for striking up friendly conversations with opposing baserunners during games:** This habit has caught the attention of several rival players. According to Freddie, even though he's trying to win, he also knows baseball is a game and wants to enjoy it, which is why he's always ready to tell someone they're doing a great job, whether that's his teammate or his opponent (Wagner, 2021).

- **Freddie was once trapped in traffic for 13 hours during a snowstorm:** Fortunately, his teammate, Chipper Jones, swooped into the rescue on an ATV! Chipper lived close by and knew exactly where to find him.
- **Freddie loved collecting baseball cards as a kid:** One of his favorites was the baseball legend Chili Davis. Freddie shared that he had collected about a hundred Chili Davis cards (Berg, 2014).

Chapter Activity: What's Your Superpower?

Have you ever wished you could have a superpower, like flying through the sky or having super strength? What if you had a special one that helped you overcome challenges? Well, in this activity, we're going to create just that!

So, grab your imagination cap and follow these steps:

1. Think about a unique superpower you wish you had. It could be something related to nature, technology, animals, or even something completely imaginative, like controlling time or reading minds. Consider how your superpower could help you overcome challenges in your own life.
2. Grab a pen and paper, and write a brief description of your superpower. Include details such as what it is, how it works, and any limitations it might have.
3. Draw a detailed illustration of your superpower. How would it look in action? Add colors and details to make your drawing come to life!

4. Write a short story or description that explains how you discovered your superpower.

5. Brainstorm ways to apply your superpower in real life. Think about specific scenarios where you would use your superpower to solve problems.

6. Consider other people too! How can your superpower help others? Maybe you could bring rain to places that really need it or make beautiful snowfalls in places where kids have never seen snow.

What awesome superpower did you come up with? Let your imagination soar! And the next time you're facing a difficult moment, remember Freddie Freeman's story and tackle it with all the strength and determination you have!

* * *

Freddie's game plan is all about going out there and swinging! How about you? How do you keep swinging toward your goals even when things get tough?

ALWAYS FIND A WAY TO BOUNCE BACK FROM SETBACKS

"A huge part of developing confidence is by working hard every day. I think that bleeds over to all aspects of anything that you're doing or working on in life."

— MIKE TROUT

Does it feel like life's throwing you a curveball lately? Maybe you're facing a setback at school, or things just haven't gone your way in sports or with friends. When these things happen, it's frustrating and can make you feel like giving up. But here's the thing: Every time life throws a challenge your way, it's also giving you an opportunity to grow stronger and more resilient.

Baseball icon Mike Trout knows a thing or two about facing tough pitches on and off the field. Before he became one of the greatest players in the game, it wasn't always smooth sailing. Just like you, he's had moments when things didn't go as planned, and those made him question if he should keep going.

But Mike didn't let those moments define him. Instead, he used them as motivation to push harder, swing stronger, and show the world what he's truly made of! Let's get to know Mike better and learn how his ability to bounce back from adversity shaped him for success.

GET TO KNOW YOUR BASEBALL HERO: MIKE TROUT

Michael "Mike" Nelson Trout was born on August 7, 1991, in Vineland, New Jersey. Mike was the youngest of three children. His parents, Jeff and Debbie, were both teachers. They encouraged all their kids to pursue their passions, whatever they might be. For Mike, that passion became clear early on: baseball.

As a kid, Mike would often ask to play catch with his friends and even slept in his Tee Ball uniform after games. He spent a lot of time at the local baseball fields, chasing down fly balls and playing with older kids. One of the coolest things he got to do was be the bat boy for the varsity team at Millville High School. As a bat boy, Mike was responsible for collecting baseballs, handing out bats to players, and cleaning up equipment. While he wasn't directly playing, he was thrilled to watch the older kids up close.

"He basically grew up in the locker room," his dad shared (Shelburne, 2010, para. 31).

When Mike was just eight years old, coaches applauded him for his ability to concentrate. They were amazed that, at his young age, he could sit through entire baseball games, watching intently without getting bored. They believed this focus would set him apart from others. True enough, by age nine, Mike was already one of the best players on a team filled with twelve-year-olds.

But why was baseball such a big part of Mike's childhood in the first place? Well, he likely inherited this passion from his dad. Jeff wasn't just a history teacher; he was also a standout baseball player in his youth. Jeff set records at Millville High School, never knowing that one day, his son would break them. He played baseball at the University of Delaware and spent four years in the Minor Leagues with the Minnesota Twins before retiring due to an injury. Understanding the challenges and uncertainties of a professional baseball career, Jeff didn't want Mike to feel pressured to follow in his footsteps. That's why, despite his deep knowledge of the game, Jeff chose not to coach his son directly. Instead, he encouraged Mike to trust his own instincts.

By the time Mike reached high school, he was already a great hitter, but his incredible speed was what truly wowed everyone. He could sprint from the batter's box to first base in less than four seconds, which was impressive for a 6-foot-2, 205-pound guy! One of his standout moments came when he was in 10th grade. In an important match against their biggest rivals, the Vineland Fighting Clan, Mike pitched masterfully, letting the opposing team only get two hits throughout the entire game. This win was particularly special because Millville hadn't beaten Vineland in years.

In 11th grade, Mike made even more progress. He pitched a no-hitter against Egg Harbor Township, striking out 18 batters! Then, in the state playoffs, his team faced Cherry Hill East. They were so afraid of Mike hitting a home run that they chose to throw pitches they knew Mike wouldn't swing at, giving him a free pass to first base every time.

Mike was so committed to baseball that instead of taking a typical summer break before his senior year, he traveled to California to compete in the Area Code Games. There, he batted impressively against some of the nation's top players. Then, during his senior year, he hit 18 home runs, setting a new high school record in New Jersey! His achievements were so remarkable that the school decided to honor him by awarding his jersey number, No. 1, to the team captain each season as a symbol of leadership and excellence (Gonzalez, 2015c).

Despite his undeniable talent, Mike was aware that professional scouts often had concerns about players from colder climates, like New Jersey, where he was from. Major League teams are worried that these players might need extra training because they couldn't play baseball during the long winter season. In fact, some other New Jersey players had struggled in the pros before, which made Mike anxious about whether any team would take a chance on him. His backup plan was to play college baseball on a scholarship at East Carolina University.

Fortunately, Mike received the news he'd been dreaming of: The Los Angeles Angels wanted him on their team! It turns out it wasn't just his skill on the field that impressed them; it was also his resilience and determination. When the scouts were watching him play, the catcher on the other team threw him out, trying to steal second base. You'd think that might discourage someone, right? Not Mike. The very next opportunity he got, he stole second base... and then stole third base right after! That kind of bounce-back attitude really caught the scouts' attention.

"You knew that when he struggled with something, it wasn't going to last very long. You knew he was going to work hard," said Greg Morhardt, the scout who made a compelling case for Mike to join the Angels. "He had that mentality of, 'I'm going to conquer this hurdle'" (Olney, 2018, para. 22).

And that's the story of how Mike went off to play pro baseball straight out of high school in 2009. He started in the Minor Leagues, and just a year later, Baseball America recognized him as the second-best overall baseball prospect. He had a stellar 2010 season and received numerous awards, including the Topps Minor League Player of the Year Award —at just 19 years old, he was the youngest player to ever achieve it! He was also named a Baseball America All-Star and a Topps Class A All-Star.

On July 8, 2011, Mike received the big news: he was promoted to the Major Leagues! At the time, he was the youngest player to debut since 2005 and the youngest for the Angels since 1971. Just a few weeks later, he hit his first Major League home run!

And the rest was history: Mike continued to impress, becoming the youngest Angel to hit two home runs in a single game on August 30—just 53 days after his first Major League game. Since then, he's been setting records and winning awards nonstop (Kiddle Encyclopedia, 2024e). Mike has been selected as an All-Star more than ten times, has earned numerous MVP awards, and is widely regarded as one of the greatest baseball players of all time!

Tough Times, Big Wins: How Mike Trout Beat the Odds!

After Mike's rookie year, he continued to establish himself as a baseball genius. And no, that's not an exaggeration— everyone claimed he had no weaknesses. Fans even often forgot how young he was because he was just that good! In fact, he became the second-youngest player ever to snag the All-Star Game's MVP award at just 22 years old, outshining other All-Stars with years of experience ahead of him. Mike was on the rise, and it seemed like nothing could stop him.

But in 2014, a major flaw showed up in Mike's game. Their opponent at the time, the Kansas City Royals, figured out during the American League Division Series that Mike had trouble hitting high fastballs! During that game, he only managed to get one hit out of twelve attempts, resulting in a devastating loss for the Angels.

Other opposing teams took note and followed suit. Mike started striking out more, finding it difficult to adjust mid-series. For the next few months, Mike saw a ton of these pitches. In June, he failed to get a single hit in 26 consecutive attempts. In July, he only managed one hit out of 25 attempts. In August, stats show that almost half of the pitches thrown to him were high fastballs, the most for any player. People started calling this his Achilles' heel, his one weakness. And it has now been exposed.

"Whaddaya know, he may be human after all," one Sports Illustrated article wrote (Jaffe, 2014, para. 12).

However, this setback didn't faze Mike. Instead, he tackled the problem like a tricky puzzle, confident he could find the solution. He spent countless hours in the batting cages, practicing against machines that fired high fastballs. But what really made the difference was adjusting how he approached each pitch. Instead of trying to anticipate when a high fastball was coming, he focused on watching each pitch closely and studying its movement. This change allowed him to react quickly in the moment.

Plus, he made a clever adjustment: with two strikes, he choked up on the bat, holding it higher up for better control. This helped him make contact with the ball more often and avoid striking out. By combining diligent practice with a new way of reading pitches, Mike was able to over-come his Kryptonite in just one offseason! When 2015 rolled in, Mike was back to being invincible. His weakness had suddenly disappeared, and opposing pitchers were stumped again.

"*Now* where do you pitch him?" Angels' bench coach Dino Ebel asked proudly (Gonzalez, 2015b, para. 4).

Mike's amazing comeback earned him his fourth Silver Slugger Award, making him only the second player to win four straight Silver Sluggers right at the start of his career. Mike's awesome season also snagged him the Best Major League Baseball Player ESPY Award!

"This dude, he refuses to lose," former Angels catcher Hank Conger shared. "His drive for everything, not only in baseball but in life, really shows what kind of player he is" (Fenno & DiGiovanna, 2014, para. 43).

Achievement Unlocked: Check Out Mike Trout's Cool Career Awards!

Because Mike refused to let setbacks stop him, he's bounced back again and again to achieve amazing things and set all sorts of records, including:

- **Baseball America Rookie of the Year Award (2012):** During his MLB debut year, Mike was named the best new player! With record-breaking performances in just his first few weeks, it came as no surprise that he earned this well-deserved award.
- **All-Star Game Most Valuable Player Award (2014, 2015):** In the All-Star Game, which brings together the best players from each MLB team, Mike was named the best of the best two times! As

of 2023, he has also been invited to compete as an All-Star a total of 11 times.

- **Youngest Member of the 100/100 Club (2015):** Only the greatest players make it into the elite 100/100 Club, where you have to hit 100 home runs and steal 100 bases before turning 25. Mike hit his 100th home run at just 23 years old, becoming the youngest player ever to reach this milestone (Gonzalez, 2015a).
- **AL MVP Awards (2014, 2016, 2019):** This award is given to the most valuable player in the American League, and Mike earned the title of MVP three times!
- **Wilson Defensive Player of the Year Award (2012, 2019):** This award goes to the best defensive player in baseball. Mike won it twice for his incredible skill at catching balls and making difficult plays look easy.

These are just a few of the awards Mike has won; he kept adding to his collection nearly every season. Among his other remarkable feats, Mike set the Angels' club record for most runs scored in a single season and the rookie record for most hits—173—in a season. He also became the first rookie ever to hit 30 home runs and steal 40 bases in just one season. In 2020, he reached a major milestone by hitting his 300th home run, surpassing the Angels' all-time record previously held by baseball legend Tim Salmon.

Additionally, a Mike Trout trading card sold for an astonishing $3.93 million at an auction, setting a new record for the most expensive sports card ever sold! It held that title until about three months later when a signed Mickey Mantle Topps trading card from 1952 sold for even more. Still, that's a huge amount of money for a trading card, particularly one featuring a player from this generation.

Apart from his skills on the field, Mike is also known for his big heart. He understands the challenges life can bring, which is why he dedicates much of his time to helping others facing difficult situations. One of the organizations he passionately supports is the Make-A-Wish Foundation, which grants wishes to children battling serious illnesses. Through this foundation, Mike has made numerous dreams come true, including those of a 7-year-old boy named Eli Velasquez. They spent a memorable day together at Angel Stadium, where Mike gifted Eli a special jersey, hit baseballs with him, and played catch on the field.

Moreover, Mike does a lot of charity work in and around his hometown. For instance, in 2022, upon learning that a family from New Jersey had lost their home to a fire, he surprised them with gifts on Christmas Eve to bring some joy during a difficult time.

"A lot of people look up to me," Mike explained, "So to be able to talk to them and give them some help, and let people know they're not alone, it means a lot to me" (Bollinger, 2023, para. 7).

This is just a glimpse of the amazing ways Mike gives back. He does so much more, which is why, in 2023, he was honored with the prestigious Roberto Clemente Award. This award is given to a player who exemplifies the spirit of baseball through exceptional character and positive impact both on and off the field, and Mike is definitely a perfect example of that!

Did You Know?

Think you know everything about your favorite player, Mike Trout? Here are some cool trivia to add to your list of fun facts:

- **Mike has been given many nicknames:** Mike has garnered a variety of nicknames throughout his career, including "Prince Fish," "God's Gift," "Millville Miracle," and "King Fish 2.0." He also earned "Millville Meteor" after an amusing incident where an anonymous vandal added it to his Wikipedia article as a joke, and the nickname stuck!

- **Mike might be able to tell you about the weather:** Even baseball prodigies have hobbies outside of the sport, and Mike's includes meteorology! In his free time, he tracks snowstorms. Someone even gifted him his very own weather balloon. Catch him occasionally as a weatherman on The Weather Channel!

- **Mike's pre-game routine involves pickles:** He has professed his love for them, even revealing that he's been munching on pickles before every game since 2017 (Sandler, 2022a).

- **Mike is what baseball fans call a "five-tool player":** That means he's amazing at hitting for average, hitting for power, base running, throwing, and fielding—basically, he's got all the skills you could ever want in a player!

- **Mike is not just a record-breaker on the field; he's also set records for how much a player gets paid:** He has signed some of the biggest contracts in baseball history. These mega-deals are a way for teams to show just how much they value Mike's amazing talent and how he's changed the entire game (Yazzie, 2024).

Chapter Activity: Challenge Accepted!

Even the greatest athletes like Mike Trout have faced setbacks, but what sets them apart from the crowd is that they found a way to bounce back stronger than ever! For this activity, you're going to think about a time when you faced a challenge and overcame it. Looking back on tough times is important because it teaches us how to do better next time, shows us how much we've grown, helps us understand ourselves better, and reminds us of just how strong we are.

So, whenever you're ready, here's what you'll do:

1. Grab your journal, a piece of paper, and a pen.
2. Find a quiet place where you can sit comfortably without distractions.
3. Think about a time when something didn't go as planned. It could be failing a test at school, not making the team, or having a disagreement with your best friend.
4. Begin by describing the setback. Write about what happened and how you felt. It's okay to be honest about your feelings. For example: "Last year, I tried out for the school soccer team but didn't make it. I felt really disappointed and sad because I had practiced a lot and really wanted to be on the team."
5. Now, think about what you did to bounce back. Did you practice more, ask for help, or try a new approach? Write down the steps you took to overcome the challenge. For example, "Instead of giving up, I decided to practice even harder. I asked my coach for tips and practiced with my friends every weekend. By the next tryout, I was much better and made the team!"
6. Then, think about what you learned from this experience. Did it make you stronger, more patient, or more determined? Write about the positive lessons you gained. For example: "I learned that hard work and persistence really pay off. I also learned not to give up, even when things don't go as planned."

7. Finish your journal entry by writing a few sentences about why bouncing back makes you strong, or include a quote that inspires resilience. You might even choose a line from your favorite song that reminds you to keep going when things get tough.

Well done! Like Mike Trout, you've proven you can conquer challenges and emerge stronger than ever. Bookmark this journal and come back to it when you need a reminder of your resilience. Remember, even if you fall seven times, you have the strength to stand up eight!

* * *

Do you take charge of your life or just go with the flow? What keeps you going when things get tough?

LEAD BY SHOWING UP EVERYDAY

"I will go every day and give everything I have, no matter what."

— FRANCISCO LINDOR

D o you ever have days when you just don't feel like doing something? Maybe it's going to school, practicing a sport, or working on a project. We all have moments like that, where we'd rather stay in bed or do something fun instead. But what if I told you that showing up, even on those tough days, can make a huge difference? That's what Francisco Lindor, or "Mr. Smile," discovered on his way to becoming a baseball icon.

Francisco Lindor plays for the New York Mets and is famous for his skills, positive attitude, and leadership on and off the field. But he didn't become great by always having easy days. Sometimes, he didn't feel like practicing either! But he learned that pushing through those moments and showing up every day, no matter what, was the key to success.

So, how did Francisco overcome those tough days and become one of the best in baseball? Let's get to know him to find out!

GET TO KNOW YOUR BASEBALL HERO: FRANCISCO LINDOR

Francisco Miguel Lindor Serrano was born on November 14, 1993, in Caguas, Puerto Rico. His parents were named Miguel and Maria, and he was the third of four kids in his family. Baseball was huge in Puerto Rico, and his dad, who loved the game, became his very first coach.

Luckily, Miguel made learning super fun. He created a game where he would stand at the top of a hill, hitting ground balls down to Francisco, who stood partway down the slope, trying to catch them. When Francisco only wanted to hit left-handed, his dad came up with a clever trick to help him get better at hitting from the right side too. Miguel would make a deal with him, saying that if Francisco hit a bucket of balls from the right side, he could then bat from the left. But there was a catch: if he missed even one ball, he had to start all over again! Little Francisco agreed to the fun challenge every time, not realizing his dad was helping him become a better player. The games were a blast, and they made Francisco fall in love with baseball.

Thanks to these moments, Francisco eventually became known as a natural switch-hitter, which became his signature trait and helped him shine in the world of pro baseball years down the line.

"To this day, the swing I have now is the exact same swing he taught me back then. It comes from him," Francisco shared (para. 22).

Growing up, Francisco had players he looked up to. There were Robbie Alomar, Omar Vizquel, Derek Jeter, Jimmy Rollins, and Barry Larkin. He dreamed of one day becoming just like them, being on TV, playing in stadiums with fans cheering. However, it was his older brother and cousin who truly motivated him to work hard. Always playing catch-up as the younger one, Francisco found himself practicing relentlessly so that he could be good enough to join their teams.

"Seeing all the things they could do on the field made me want to improve every single day," Francisco recalled (Lindor, 2019, para 17).

When Francisco was 12 years old, he left Puerto Rico with his dad and flew to the United States to study at Montverde Academy, a boarding school located in Florida, where he played as a shortstop—a defensive player who stands between second and third base. In his senior year, he had quite the season. He maintained an impressive batting average, brought in 13 runs for his team, and hit six home runs that all flew out of the park! His performance was so amazing that it caught the eyes of many people, including universities and reporters. He was offered a full scholarship to play at Florida State and was even recognized by USA Today as one of the most outstanding high school baseball athletes.

Then, in 2011, just when Francisco was about to start college, the Cleveland Indians offered him a chance to play baseball professionally for them! It was a dream come true, so of course, he jumped at the chance. And the rest, as they say, is history. Since then, Francisco has become a well-known figure in Major League Baseball. He's been named an All-Star and has won both the Silver Slugger Award and the Gold Glove Award multiple times!

The moment Francisco stepped onto the professional baseball scene, fans immediately noticed the special energy he brought to the field. It was the same attitude he had when he was just a kid playing baseball with his brother and cousin in Puerto Rico. Instead of playing with intensity and aggressiveness like other athletes, Francisco showed up with genuine curiosity, bright eyes, and a big smile. He was always quick to give high-fives, jump with excitement, and spread joy. That's why everyone started calling him Mr. Smile! Francisco didn't mind his new nickname, though.

"I think the world's a beautiful place, and people should get along," he once said. "That's one of the reasons I love to smile. You can smile to someone and you can brighten their day 'cause smiling's infectious" (Serby, 2023, para. 4).

Tough Times, Big Wins: How Francisco Lindor Beat the Odds!

Behind Francisco's bright smile and infectious energy on the MLB field, there was a lot he had to overcome early on. He once shared that moving from Puerto Rico to the United States was one of the hardest challenges he had ever faced.

"That period was by far the most challenging of my life," he recalled (Lindor, 2019, para. 34).

His dad brought Francisco with him to Florida to support his MLB dreams by enrolling him in Montverde Academy, a boarding school famous for its sports programs. His dad thought Francisco would benefit from learning a new language, experiencing a different culture, and competing against even better baseball players there. Francisco's dad had already moved to the U.S., so he was physically there to support him. However, his mom and older siblings had to stay in Puerto Rico, making the transition scary and over-whelming for young Francisco. He missed his mom's cooking almost immediately—those delicious pork chops, beans, and empanadas.

"She's the best cook," Francisco shared (para. 12).

Without his family, friends, and favorite foods, everything felt unfamiliar. Then, his dad took him to Montverde Academy, which Francisco described as being "in a small town in the middle of nowhere," where he would be staying. Living apart from his parents and starting at a new school where he didn't know anyone made Francisco feel extremely lonely. The experience forced him to grow up quickly.

"Your mom is not there to help you with your homework or your laundry," he explained. "When you have nothing to eat and you're trying to find something to eat, you have to make something in your microwave" (Meisel, 2015, para. 28).

The biggest obstacle Francisco faced during this time was the language barrier. He was an extremely talkative kid, and back in Puerto Rico, he chatted with people all the time in Spanish. Meanwhile, in Florida, where most of his school-mates spoke English, he couldn't understand anyone, and they couldn't understand him. When his dad dropped him off for the first day of school, he had Francisco memorize the phrase "I don't understand." But Francisco just couldn't remember it, so his dad wrote it in the palm of his hand instead. Every time someone would talk to him in English that day, he would just show them his hand. This made Francisco feel totally uncool.

Baseball, something that used to be second nature to him, also became a challenge. At just 13 years old, Francisco was placed on the varsity team. He had to compete against much older players, most of whom were 17 or 18 years old. They were stronger, taller, and better than him. During his first game with them, he grabbed the shortest bat he could find and struggled to swing even that! Francisco felt like a loser even on the field where he used to shine the best. At Montverde Academy, everything was strange, and Francisco didn't fit in anywhere.

To keep Francisco strong and motivated, his dad continu-ously reminded him that these experiences would help him grow both as a person and as a baseball player and could bring him opportunities he might not have had back home. Francisco knew deep down that he was lucky to have this chance, which not many kids get. So, even though he felt scared and wanted to just hide in his room, he decided to show up and try his best every day.

The first thing he focused on was learning English. At the time, Francisco was already enrolled in an English as a Second Language (ESL) class. However, in an attempt to look cool, he didn't take it seriously. He acted as though he didn't care about learning English because he was actually afraid that other kids would tease him for trying. But when everyone in the class advanced to the next level, and he was the only one held back after the first semester, he realized he needed to change.

"I was like, *Oh, hold up. I've got to take this serious. This is not cool anymore*," He remembered thinking to himself. "I'm the only one sitting in this classroom. This is actually very embarrassing" (Schreffler, 2023, para. 23).

That's when Francisco started paying close attention to everything around him, asking questions, and doing whatever he could to learn. He took summer classes and used Google to look up things on his own. He realized that the school staff and teachers were extremely kind, as they helped him make progress. Francisco tackled his goal step-by-step. And even though it took some time, within a year and a half, he could speak English.

Francisco was back on track! He enjoyed going to classes again now that he could understand the lessons. He started chatting about movies and music with his classmates too.

Best of all, he was able to make new friends. This fresh confidence not only helped his grades but also his performance on the baseball field. He socialized more with his teammates, played better than ever, and felt like he finally truly belonged.

"Everything I did on the baseball diamond became about joy again. And fun," Francisco shared (Lindor, 2019, para. 41).

It was a good thing he kept showing up! This consistency is something Francisco carried with him well into his Major League years. He became known for his dedication. Even when he wasn't feeling his best, he never missed a practice or a game. He believed that showing up every day and making small, steady improvements was better than not trying at all.

"Consistency is something extremely important in anything you do, in baseball, in being a brother, being a son, being a dad," Francisco shared. "Anything you do you got to be consistent. And you got to stay positive" (Stance, n.d., para. 14).

Achievement Unlocked: Check Out Francisco Lindor's Cool Career Awards!

Francisco Lindor's story proves that showing up every day with determination and a cheerful attitude can lead to amazing achievements. Thanks to his dedication and positivity, he earned several awards, including:

- **MLB Rookie of the Month Award (2015):** In his very first month playing Major League Baseball, Francisco was recognized as the top newcomer in the league!

- **American League Silver Slugger Award (2017) and National League (2023):** This award celebrates the best hitters, and Francisco proved he was one of the best in both leagues!

- **Bob Feller Man of the Year Award (2018):** This award honors players who excel both on and off the field. Francisco was recognized for his leadership, sportsmanship, and positive influence, making him a great role model for fans and teammates.

- **Cleveland Indians Heart and Hustle Award (2019):** Given to players who show great effort and enthusiasm, Francisco won this award in 2019 for his dedication and energy, both on and off the field.

- **Marvin Miller Man of the Year Award (2022):** This award honors players who make a huge impact on the game and their community. Francisco received it for his leadership and positive contributions.

- **Joe DiMaggio "Toast of the Town" Award (2023):** Celebrating players who bring excitement and joy to the game, Francisco earned this award in 2023 for being a standout player and fan favorite (*Francisco Lindor Awards*, n.d.).

These are just a few of the amazing awards Francisco has received, and there are many more. It's clear that Francisco's diligence and optimism made a huge difference, not just in his own life but also in MLB. If he hadn't shown up day after day and kept pushing through, we might not have one of the most exciting and charming players to watch today!

Did You Know?

Think you know everything about your favorite player, Francisco Lindor? Here are some cool trivia to add to your list of fun facts:

- **Francisco answers with another nickname:** In addition to Mr. Smile, which he proudly wears on his jersey, people also call him Paquito. In Spanish, Paquito is a sweet and affectionate way of saying Francisco, so that's what his mom calls him—how cute!

- **Francisco made history for his home country:** In 2016, he became the first Puerto Rican shortstop to ever win the Gold Glove Award in the MLB, a prestigious honor recognizing the best defensive players. And because one Gold Glove wasn't enough, he went on to win another one in 2019 (Puma, 2021).

- **There's a building named after Francisco:** Thanks to Francisco's support, Montverde Academy has a brand-new middle school building named "Lindor Hall." It's filled with exciting features like athletic offices, a showcase of the school's sports awards, and state-of-the-art training facilities. There's also an entire field named after him! Now, when Francisco visits the school—something he is known to love doing—these moments will be even more special as he sees a reflection of his journey in the very place that helped shape his talents (Colby, 2021).

- **Francisco loves trying new things:** During the 2018 offseason, he took a break from baseball to dive into something new—Aikido, a Japanese martial art. He even traveled to Tokyo to learn the moves. Talk about dedication!

- **Francisco used to wear braces:** Before he became known for his bright, confident smile, Francisco was a bit shy about showing his teeth. He shared that once his braces came off, he felt a boost in confidence and loved smiling even more. He even considered becoming a dentist at one point (Kaneko, 2018).

Chapter Activity: The Consistency Challenge: Get to Know Your Baseball Hero: Anthony Rizzo

When Francisco was just starting out, he faced a lot of challenges, but he never gave up! He knew that by showing up and doing his best everyday, he could get better and achieve his goals. So, for this activity, we're going to try to be consistent and reliable, just like him.

How? Just follow these simple steps:

1. First, think about something you really want to get better at. It could be anything—playing a musical instrument, practicing a sport, helping out around

the house more, or maybe learning a new language, just like Francisco did when he was 12 years old.

2. Grab a calendar, or ask your parents for one. Write down your goal at the top and decide how many days a week you're going to work on it. Showing up every day is key, so try to make it a daily activity if you can.

3. Every day you work toward your goal, put up a sticker or mark the day with a colored marker. This will help you see how often you're showing up.

4. At the end of each week, look at your calendar. How many days did you show up? Celebrate your progress, no matter how small. Every little bit counts!

Remember, just as Francisco said, being consistent isn't just about sports, school, or big dreams—it's about everything you do. That includes being a good friend, helping your family, and even being kind to yourself.

* * *

What are you going to show up for today?

ENDURE CHALLENGES BY BELIEVING IN YOURSELF

"I believe that everything you work at and want in life is a great challenge."

— ANTHONY RIZZO

Have you ever had times when everything seemed clouded in doubt? Maybe you had to take a break from school or sports because you were dealing with an illness, or perhaps your family went through changes, and you had to get used to new living arrangements. It's in these moments that being strong and believing in yourself can truly make a big difference.

This same resilience and self-belief worked for Anthony Rizzo, a baseball icon celebrated for his infectious spirit. Affectionately called Tony, he lived by a simple mantra:

Create your own weather! He has endured challenges that were daunting and sometimes made his life messy, but he always managed to overcome them and come out on top. Let's learn more about Tony and discover how he maintains his optimism during tough times!

GET TO KNOW YOUR BASEBALL HERO: ANTHONY RIZZO

Anthony "Tony" Vincent Rizzo was born on August 8, 1989, in Fort Lauderdale, Florida. Baseball was a huge part of the Rizzo household. When Tony and his older brother, John Jr., turned five years old, their parents signed them up for Little League. Their dad, John, had loved playing Little League as a kid and was eager to pass on the excitement to his sons. That's why, despite his busy programming career, he stepped up to coach his kids' team. Meanwhile, their mom, Laurie, who also worked full-time as a bartender, supported her boys by managing the team and ensuring no one ever ran out of snacks.

While Tony's dad-slash-coach was committed to teaching every kid on the team not just baseball but also teamwork, respect, and other important life lessons, the number one priority was always to have fun. And John and Laurie knew exactly how to do that: ice cream! If the team won, they got ice cream as a reward after the game. And if the team lost... well, they got ice cream anyway. They called this the "Ice cream if you win. Ice cream if you lose" rule.

"Anthony is still eating ice cream before and after games now. A lot of it," his dad shared (McCormick, 2017, para. 5).

The fun didn't just stay on the field; it spilled over into their home. Despite Mom Laurie's ban on indoor baseball, the boys couldn't resist grabbing their gear when it was just the three of them. Of course, this sometimes resulted in broken lamps, but the memories they created were absolutely priceless.

It's no wonder both Tony and his brother kept their athletic spirit alive long after they outgrew Little League at age 12. Tony's older brother focused on football in high school, eventually landing a full-ride scholarship to play college football at Florida Atlantic University. Meanwhile, Tony decided to stick to baseball while studying at Marjory Stoneman Douglas High School.

He started pitching for the varsity team in 11th grade, but his first game was a rough one. He struggled so much that the first eight players from the other team all made it to first base. Instead of getting discouraged, Tony decided to use the experience as a chance to learn. In fact, just three days later, he immediately showed how much he'd improved by striking out batters one by one with ease!

"I wouldn't have thought so at the time," Tony explained. "Now, I can say it probably helped me in the long run. I grew from it" (Moshier, 2013, para. 2).

Tony's impressive performance continued throughout the season, ending with three wins, zero losses, and five saves. By his senior year, Tony had become the team's star pitcher. He won ten games, lost only one, and allowed very few runs, establishing himself as one of the best pitchers in the area!

But Tony has always been a level-headed kid, knowing it's smart not to put all your eggs in one basket. That's why, in addition to being an athlete, he was also determined to become a biomedical engineer. In fact, he had his sights set on Florida Atlantic University, which offered him a scholarship to major in physics when the Boston Red Sox came in and offered him a spot on their team in 2007! Tony faced a tough decision between two exciting paths. Ultimately, he chose his first love: baseball.

And that's how Tony kicked off his career as a professional baseball player. Since then, he's been named an All-Star, earned numerous awards, and even reigned as a World Series champ!

Tough Times, Big Wins: How Anthony Rizzo Beat the Odds!

Tony was on top of the world. He had just graduated from high school and was now living his baseball dream at just 18 years old. But then, out of nowhere, something felt off. In April 2008, after returning from a fun road trip with friends, his legs and ankles swelled up so much that it caused him to gain 15 pounds! When the swelling didn't clear up after a couple of days, his teammates became alarmed, and one of them told Tony's dad.

John immediately fetched his son and rushed him to doctors in South Carolina and Boston. After several tests and anxious waiting, the news came back—one of the hardest things a young athlete, or anyone, could ever hear: It was cancer. Specifically, one called "Hodgkin's lymphoma."

"It was definitely very shocking," Tony shared. "I was 18 years old and on top of the world, playing professional baseball while all of my friends were off at college. I had no idea what cancer was" (Miller, 2021, para. 9).

The gut-wrenching news deeply affected those close to Tony. To make matters worse, his grandma was battling a different type of cancer too. It was a tough time for the whole Rizzo household, but they found strength in sticking together.

"I realized that cancer is so much more than individual hardship, but rather a battle that the whole family must face together," Tony wrote about the experience afterward (Rizzo, n.d.).

His teammates at the Boston Red Sox were devastated but also eager to support Tony, so they summoned him to Fenway Park to meet with the team's general manager, Theo Epstein. The atmosphere was tense that day. Everyone felt a bit panicked and worried about Tony. Yet, true to form, when Tony arrived, he brought his own weather with him.

"When Anthony showed up, he was almost like the calming influence," Theo shared (Cassavell, 2015, para. 8).

Theo then introduced the rookie Tony to Jon Lester, a seasoned Red Sox pitcher. The reason for this meeting was simple: Jon had battled cancer himself two years prior and had overcome it. The two spent about an hour talking. Tony was grateful that Jon didn't treat him like a frightened patient, although he admitted that that's exactly how he felt. Instead, Jon treated him like a teammate facing a tough opponent. When Jon shared his own battle with cancer, he framed it as a difficult baseball match he was determined to win.

Jon also assured Tony that this wasn't the end of his MLB career—that he could and would bounce back; he just had to focus on getting better. To show Tony he was telling the truth, just a few days after their talk, Jon pitched a flawless no-hitter! Tony actually fainted from relief after hearing Jon's encouraging words.

"It was everything I needed to hear," Tony explained. "I was thinking the same thing: *I have to do whatever it takes to get this out of me.* He beat his cancer; I knew I could too" (Sanchez, 2016, para. 24.)

And so Tony started chemotherapy, the medical treatment he had to undergo for six months. Chemotherapy was tough; it made him feel nauseous and drained his energy. There were days when he didn't want to leave the house, and he gained weight quickly as a side effect.

"It wasn't fun," Tony shared. "The only thing I ate was my mom's pasta and her sauce. If I were really nauseous, I would drink a milkshake or eat brownies" (Smith, 2013, paras. 46, 48).

Despite these challenges, Tony held onto Jon's advice—to keep living his life and not let cancer control it. So, he continued doing things he loved whenever he could. He spent time with his family and friends, finding joy in everyday moments and keeping his spirits up. Even when doubts crept in about his future in baseball, Tony pushed through, determined to overcome cancer and return to the sport he loved so much stronger than ever.

In September of that same year, as the Rizzo family was preparing to board a plane to watch his older brother play football at Florida Atlantic University, Tony's mom, Laurie, received a call from his doctor. They heard the word they had all been hoping and praying for: remission. That means that the doctors couldn't find any more cancer cells in Tony's body after all the treatments and care. Tony cried and hugged his family, overwhelmed with gratitude.

"Just hearing the news was awesome. The tumors were fully gone," Laurie recalled (Cassavell, 2015, para. 15).

It was an important moment that marked the end of a difficult period in their lives and the beginning of Tony's comeback! In 2010, he finally felt well enough to return to the diamond, and since then, his career has been nothing short of remarkable. He kept grinding in the Minor Leagues with the Boston Red Sox, where he snagged the title of Minor League Offensive Co-Player of the Year.

His skills caught attention fast, leading to a trade to the San Diego Padres in 2011. With his new team, he made waves right away, earning awards like the Padres' Minor League Player of the Month for April, May, and June. Baseball America then dubbed him San Diego's number-one prospect.

That same year, Tony finally got his shot in the Major Leagues! After his debut game, while he was being interviewed by reporters, his teammates surprised him with a pie to the face—a welcome tradition for every rookie! Despite being covered in cream, Tony had the biggest smile.

""I'm like a little kid right now," he said. "I'm just honored to be here. It's been a fun ride so far" (Togerson, 2011, para. 7).

In 2012, Tony got traded to the Chicago Cubs, where he earned several recognitions, including the National League Rookie of the Month for July and the Cubs' Player of the Month for September. In 2013, he played internationally, representing Team Italy in the World Baseball Classic. His great-grandparents were from Sicily, and both his parents are of Italian descent. For Tony, playing for Team Italy was a way to connect with his heritage and experience a unique sense of pride. Despite the initial language barrier, he quickly learned how to communicate and work well with his teammates.

"Baseball is baseball," he explained (MLB, 2013, para. 4).

Tony played a huge role in the team's success, earning him the title of National Italian American Sports Hall of Fame Athlete of the Year! The team's victory was so impressive that it shook up the sports scene in Italy, putting baseball back in the headlines in a country where soccer usually steals the spotlight. Suddenly, everyone was talking about baseball again, thanks to Tony and Team Italy's incredible performance.

Tony kept making waves in 2014. He received a staggering 8.8 million votes to win the MLB All-Star Final Vote, securing his spot in the MLB All-Star Game for the first time.

But Tony's biggest moment came in 2016, when he led the Chicago Cubs to their first World Series Championship in over a century—yes, over a hundred years!

And what was Tony like as a leader, you may ask? As always, he brought his own infectious energy! Before key games in the World Series, Tony did something funny: he delivered motivational speeches completely naked! Channeling the spirit of Rocky Balboa, a legendary underdog boxer from the movies, he quoted Rocky's famous lines and even shadow-boxed to inspire his team ("Anthony Rizzo Was Naked When He Made His Motivational Speeches," 2017).

His antics brought laughter, eased everyone's nerves, and never failed to fire up the team. It's this type of energy and optimism that carried Tony through everything, whether he was facing a tough opponent on the baseball diamond or battling cancer off it. Tony truly brings sunshine wherever he goes.

Achievement Unlocked: Check Out Anthony Rizzo's Cool Career Awards!

Tony's incredible story teaches us a powerful lesson: No matter what obstacles you face, believing in yourself and staying optimistic are the keys to overcoming them. It's thanks to this mindset that Tony received multiple awards and broke a number of records, including:

- **Branch Rickey Award (2014):** The Branch Rickey Award celebrates players who not only perform well on the field but also help their communities in amazing ways. Tony earned this award because he's not only an amazing player, but he also strives to make a positive impact beyond baseball.

- **Heart and Hustle Award (2015):** This award celebrates players who show immense passion and determination on the field. Tony got this award because that's totally him—always giving his all!
- **Gold Glove Award (2016, 2018, 2019, 2020):** Tony's amazing skills at first base earned him several Gold Glove Awards!
- **The Silver Slugger Award (2016):** Tony's batting skills were so impressive that he got this award, proving he's one of the best hitters in the National League.
- **Marvin Miller Man of the Year Award (2017):** Tony was honored with this award for his leadership and charity work. This award shows how he's making a big difference in the world!
- **Roberto Clemente Award (2017):** Tony earned this award for being the Most Valuable Person at making the world a better place *(Anthony Rizzo Awards,* n.d.).

These awards only scratch the surface of Tony's achievements; there are plenty more where these came from. As you can see, the recognitions he received highlight not just his skills on the field but also his impact on the community. That's because he has turned his most difficult experience into a driving force for supporting others facing similar challenges.

During his battle with cancer, Tony saw how deeply it affected not just himself but everyone he loved. That's when he made a promise to his mom that once he's all better, he's going to start a foundation to help other families going through cancer.

"That's the person he always was," his mom shared. "I can remember when he went on a field trip in elementary school and used the money I gave him to buy a gift for a kid who was home sick that day" (Santasiere III, 2024).

True to his word, in 2012, Tony founded the Anthony Rizzo Family Foundation. Its mission is to raise money for cancer research and provide support to children and their families fighting this disease. They organize cool events like the Walk-Off for Cancer 5K, where hundreds of people meet up to run and walk while raising millions of dollars. Using these funds, the Anthony Rizzo Family Foundation teams up with hospitals to ensure that kids with cancer and their families receive the best possible care. This means they can focus on supporting each other without stressing about paying for things like medicine, treatments, or groceries (Kiddle Encyclopedia, 2024a).

"Battling a life-threatening illness gave me the resilience and tenacity to go after my dreams," Tony explained. "It is my honor and privilege to support other young warriors and families in their time of need" (*New York Yankees First Baseman*, 2023, para. 2).

In 2020, Tony also gave back to Marjory Stoneman Douglas High School by helping upgrade the school's baseball and softball fields with brand-new lights. Now, students could practice and play games long after the sun went down. To show their appreciation, they renamed the baseball field "Anthony Rizzo Field." If it were up to Tony, it would probably always be bright in there!

Did You Know?

Think you know everything about your favorite player, Anthony Rizzo? Here are some cool trivia to add to your list of fun facts:

- **Tony discovered a new talent in 2016:** During his spare time at Spring Training, he started learning how to play the piano. And he has gotten quite good at it! You can sometimes catch him posting covers of popular songs on Instagram.
- **Tony has a summertime treat named after him:** Remember his parents' "Ice cream if you win. Ice cream if you lose" rule? They always headed to Lyndhurst Pastry Shop after games to keep that promise. To honor their family tradition, the shop named an ice cream after him: the "Anthony Rizzo." It's a yummy mix of half chocolate and half vanilla (Sandler, 2022b).
- **Tony's Italian-American roots shine through his love for food, especially dishes rooted in Sicilian tradition:** Growing up, his family always cooked together. A favorite meal that still holds a special place in his heart to this day is pasta with sauce paired with chicken cutlets. Sounds delicious!

- **Like many athletes, Tony gets superstitious during important games:** Take the 2016 National League Championship Series, for example. He accidentally broke his phone but refused to get it fixed because he was absolutely terrified it might jinx the Cubs' winning streak.
- **In his high school yearbook, Tony quoted legendary football coach Vince Lombardi:** "It's not whether you get knocked down, it's whether you get up." This shows Tony had always had incredible self-belief, even way back then (Pisano, 2016).

Chapter Activity: My Weather Map

Even the greatest athletes, like Anthony Rizzo, know that life can have its ups and downs. The secret to overcoming tough times is to believe in yourself and "create your own weather." This means staying positive and strong, no matter what challenges come your way. In this activity, you'll create your own weather map to help you stay positive on dreary days!

When you're ready, follow these simple steps:

1. Grab some paper and your favorite coloring supplies—crayons, markers, or colored pencils.
2. Think about the challenges you are currently facing. Write down some of them on a piece of paper. It could be dealing with an illness or injury,

facing mean classmates, or any other tough situation you are dealing with right now.

3. Draw a big picture of yourself in the center of the paper.

4. Around your picture, draw rain clouds.

5. Inside each rain cloud, write down one of the challenges you listed. These rain clouds represent the tough times you're facing right now.

6. Then, think about the things that can help you stay positive and strong. These could be family, friends, or hobbies.

7. Around each rain cloud, draw a rainbow or another symbol that represents how you plan to overcome the challenge. For example, if your family helps you stay positive, draw a rainbow or heart near that rain cloud. If playing a sport makes you feel strong, draw a soccer ball or bat near another rain cloud.

8. Use your coloring supplies to decorate your weather map. Make it colorful and fun! Add more symbols and drawings that make you happy and remind you of your strengths.

And you're done! Put your weather map somewhere you can see it every day, like on your bedroom wall or the fridge. This way, whenever you're feeling down, you can look at it and remember how strong and resilient you are. Remember, when you believe in yourself, you can overcome anything!

* * *

Have you ever felt like you couldn't do something? How did you start believing in yourself again?

STAY STRONG AND KEEP GOING, NO MATTER WHAT

"If you don't have dreams, you don't have a life."

— BRYCE HARPER

Have you ever felt like every move you make toward your dreams is met with doubt from others? Maybe you've been told your ideas won't work, that you're making mistakes, or that you're not good enough. Bryce Harper, well-known as one of the greatest baseball players of our era, knows this struggle all too well. Since he was young, Bryce has faced countless people questioning his choices and critiquing his character.

Despite this, Bryce's focus and drive to be the best have always prevailed. Instead of letting negativity hold him back, Bryce used it as motivation to prove the doubters wrong. He has never allowed anything or anyone to distract him from his goals. He stayed strong and kept going. Let's learn more about Bryce to see how he developed this laser focus and unstoppable willpower!

GET TO KNOW YOUR BASEBALL HERO: BRYCE HARPER

Bryce Aron Max Harper was born on October 16, 1992, in Las Vegas, Nevada. His dad, Ron, worked with heavy steel, and his mom, Sheri, worked in the legal field. They first noticed Bryce's love for baseball when he was just three years old. At that young age, Bryce was already swinging his T-ball bat and playing against older kids. How adorable!

Bryce's path to greatness began somewhere unexpected: right in the family garage. Every day, when his dad came home from work, Bryce would excitedly ask him to throw balls for him to hit. His dad could never refuse and always ended up saying yes. They would set up a net and spend countless hours practicing together. Ron even pitched unusual things like sunflower seeds, bottle caps, and dried red beans to help Bryce improve his hand-eye coordination.

When asked how many times his dad pitched to him during these sessions, Bryce said, "Millions. Absolutely millions" (Mercury News, 2016, para. 9).

That's probably why, at age seven, Bryce was already ahead of his peers. He joined a travel baseball team called the Ballbusters, where he played up to 130 games per year across many states—so many that he lost count! That's when Bryce started getting really popular because of his advanced skills. It was also when he first encountered negative opinions, especially about his parents.

Sometimes, his parents came along to his out-of-state games, but other times, due to work schedules or financial limitations, Bryce had to travel alone with his coach and teammates. Because of that, some people thought of them as bad parents. They also claimed that Bryce was missing out on his childhood because his parents let him play too much baseball. They said he should be doing more "typical kid stuff" instead of traveling so much. But Bryce knew they just didn't understand; there was no such thing as too much baseball! So, he shrugged off their comments.

"He loves to play baseball," Mom Sheri explained. "He would come home after being away playing baseball all weekend, get off the plane and not an hour later be bored and say, 'Dad, let's go to the cage and hit'" (Verducci, 2009, para. 30).

But while Bryce played on the field for fun, he approached practice with a seriousness uncommon for kids his age. For instance, in one memorable game, Bryce hit an inside fastball that flew foul for what felt like miles! After that, opponents started throwing tricky pitches at him (Clary, 2015). This motivated Bryce to work even harder during batting practice with his dad, strategizing and refining his swing. In a short amount of time, he had learned to hit all kinds of pitches and cover every part of the field purely by instinct!

"I know I worked every single day. I know I did as much as I could with my dad," Bryce recalled (Kilgore, n.d., para. 5).

In high school, Bryce attended Las Vegas High. He excelled not just in baseball but also in football, basketball, and snowboarding. However, it was obvious that baseball was number one in his heart. In fact, he would sneak into the batting cage between football practice and classes, still dressed in his padded football gear.

"I can't remember a time when Bryce didn't have big calluses on his hands from hitting," shared Tanner Chauncey, Bryce's childhood friend. "He was working when the rest of us weren't" (Keown, 2016, para. 9).

As his skills progressed, so did his popularity. When he was 13 years old, while participating in a tournament called Rocket City in Alabama, Bryce recalled seeing every person in the stadium turn their heads all at the same time to look at him, cheering his name. Then, at 16, Bryce hit an incredible 502-foot home run at Tropicana Field in St. Petersburg, Florida—the longest ever recorded at the Tampa Bay Rays' home ballpark! Soon enough, Sports Illustrated had his picture on the cover, dubbing him "Baseball's Chosen One." They even compared him to basketball genius LeBron James —a pretty big deal!

His high school coach, Sam Thomas, wasn't surprised at all. In fact, long before Bryce joined his team, Sam had seen him play at a youth camp he ran when Bryce was just six years old. Even then, Bryce stood out from the crowd.

"You always have kids that are people-pleasers," Sam shared. "But Bryce at that age wanted to do everything, and he had a way about him that said, 'I'm going to do it, and I'm going to do it better than everyone'" (Brookover, 2019).

Deep down, Bryce's dream wasn't just to play pro baseball; he wanted to be the best player baseball's ever had. He was shooting for the top, and he wasn't shy about letting everyone know. Thanks to this mindset and his seriously impressive work ethic, he earned Baseball America's High School Player of the Year award in 10th grade (Frommer, 2024). Inspired by these early successes, Bryce set another ambitious goal: To reach the Major Leagues by age 18 or 19 —a few years earlier than most players do!

To achieve this goal, Bryce had a plan. In 11th grade, he decided to get his General Educational Development (GED) certificate, which meant finishing high school early so he could enter the MLB draft sooner. While most kids were thinking about prom and summer vacations, Bryce was studying hard, practicing with his dad and coach every day, and planning his future in pro baseball. He turned down many party invitations so he could spend more time working toward his goal. The result? Bryce succeeded in obtaining his GED! His loved ones never doubted him for a second and were so proud of what he had achieved.

However, right in the midst of the celebration, some sports writers were arguing in the papers that he was making a huge mistake by focusing on baseball. They suggested he should instead continue high school and start considering another career path, just in case baseball didn't work out.

They even questioned why his parents supported his decision. Imagine being an 11th grader and seeing in the news that adult sports experts thought you were making all the wrong choices and making your mom and dad appear like they were bad parents!

But, unlike the critics, Bryce didn't have any doubt he'd make it as a pro baseball player. The only question for him was how he was going to make it happen. Plus, he was so used to other people telling him to be more realistic by then. One time, in 6th grade, even the nice lady heading Career Day told him to pick a new dream after he shared that what he wanted to be was a pro baseball player. So, he once again chose to ignore their opinions and stayed focused on what's ahead of him: college baseball!

The following year, he enrolled at the College of Southern Nevada. Though he was mostly a hitter, the Southern Nevada Coyotes placed him as a catcher so he could become an all-around player faster. The coolest part was that he was on the team with his older brother, Bryan, who was a starting pitcher. They made an awesome duo!

Bryce's performance at the College of Southern Nevada was truly remarkable. In 66 games, he hit 31 home runs and drove in 98 runs! His 31 home runs shattered the school's previous record of 12, earning him the 2010 Scenic West Athletic Conference (SWAC) Player of the Year award. In the Western district finals of the 2010 National Junior College Athletic Association (NJCAA) World Series, Bryce put on a show, getting six hits out of seven. The next day, he went a perfect 6-for-6. Among those, he hit 4 home runs and also made it to both third and second base, helping the team score more points.

Now that many more people were watching him play, Bryce faced even more scrutiny. This time, it was about his fiery and competitive personality. Unlike most players, Bryce was very vocal about wanting to win.

"I respect everyone on the field," Bryce once said. "But if you're on the other team, even if we're buddies, I'm trying to beat you" (Sheinin, 2011, para. 30).

One notable incident occurred during the National Junior College World Series, where he was ejected from a game for arguing with the umpire about a so-called third strike. As he walked away, Bryce used his bat to draw a line in the dirt, showing where he thought the pitch should have been. Officials didn't appreciate this gesture and thought he was being rude. This resulted in a two-game suspension. He was asked to leave the field and stop playing for his team. His team lost that game and the next one, leading to their elimination from the tournament.

After this, some reporters blamed Bryce for the team's loss. Moreover, they started saying that Bryce's actions could mess up his budding career. Many began to doubt if any team would want to take a chance on a player known for being too brash. There were even whispers that Bryce wouldn't be drafted by the major teams at all.

On the other hand, many baseball fans believed that the punishment was way too harsh and that Bryce had the right to voice his opinions. It was a hot topic, with people on both sides arguing about whether Bryce would go on to become a star or if his career might end there. It seemed like a big question mark hung over his future in baseball.

Bryce felt awful, not because of what people were saying, but because he knew he had let his team down—a mistake he was determined never to repeat. He was so regretful that he couldn't sleep. In fact, his coach, Tim Chambers, woke up to a text from Bryce the next day, sent just after midnight. It read: *I love you coach! I'm sorry!* (Sheinin, 2011)

And Coach Tim was right! While Bryce often looked confident, he was actually dealing with a level of pressure that most kids—and even adults—could hardly imagine. Here he was, just a teenager, facing pitchers in their twenties who were throwing lightning-fast 90-mile-per-hour fastballs. Plus, Bryce wasn't just playing for himself; he wanted to take care of his family and help his dad stop working in the iron mill too. With thousands of fans in the stands and even more watching from home, every move he made was under intense scrutiny. The weight of all of these expectations sometimes made Bryce feel overwhelmed and scared. There were moments when he felt like giving up entirely, and he even once considered going back to high school, even though that wasn't an option anymore.

With everything he had worked for on the line, Bryce knew he had to stay strong and focused. Fortunately, despite the naysayers, his skills remained undeniable, and he was even awarded the 2010 Golden Spikes Award that year! This award is given to the best amateur baseball player in the whole country. Bryce's also proved the doubters wrong when he achieved his goal and was drafted in the Major Leagues by the Washington Nationals that same year! To celebrate, he chose to wear jersey number 34, explaining that he had always admired the legendary baseball player Mickey Mantle while growing up. Combining 3 and 4 equaled Mickey's number 7.

Since then, Bryce has consistently excelled. Today, he stands as an MLB All-Star, a former National League MVP, and a three-time winner of the Silver Slugger Award (Kiddle Encyclopedia, 2024b).

"The pressure's all behind me. This is what I love to do," Bryce once shared (O'Shea, 2023, para. 54).

His dedication to the game has made him one of the most respected players in baseball. It's amazing to think it all began with hitting red beans and sunflower seeds in their family garage. Who could've known? Well, Bryce sure did! And, thankfully, he stuck to his gut despite what everyone else said.

Tough Times, Big Wins: How Bryce Harper Beats the Odds!

Even though Bryce Harper is considered a baseball genius, he faced challenges just like anyone else. One major unexpected hurdle? His eyesight! He noticed it during a game when he suddenly struggled to hit. So, he visited a doctor. It turned out he had seriously poor eyesight. His doctor even said it was one of the worst cases he had ever seen, and he wondered how Bryce had been able to hit a ball before. After being prescribed contact lenses, Bryce was back on the field and playing better than ever. But imagine being so good at batting that it took you such a long time to notice you actually had blurry vision.

Years later, another big obstacle came his way. While playing right field, Bryce made a powerful throw from the outfield to home plate, trying to stop a run, when suddenly he felt a sharp pain in his right elbow. Later, it was discovered that he tore the UCL in his throwing arm. The UCL helps stabilize the elbow during throwing motions, and Bryce's tear meant he couldn't throw without risking more damage. When the public found out about his injury, many people thought his season was over because most players needed surgery right away. But Bryce wasn't like most players, as we already know. Instead, he surprised everyone by deciding to continue what he set out to do, which was to keep hitting for the rest of the year. Despite the injury, Bryce's performance and numbers continued to be impressive. He also kept his spirits up.

"I'm good, just hit my funny bone," he joked in an interview (Wilson, 2023, para. 5).

After the season, Bryce finally decided to undergo surgery to fix his arm. This surgery usually requires a long recovery time, typically taking over a year. The healing process often involves several months of intensive rehabilitation and physical therapy. So, typical Bryce, he went ahead and set a new goal: To get back on the field earlier than was typical.

True to form, Bryce's determination propelled him back onto the field ahead of schedule! In just 159 days—less than six months—he made an incredible comeback, setting a new record for the fastest return from this type of injury in Major League Baseball (ESPN News Services, 2023). A strange achievement to have, really, but trust Bryce to be the one to earn it. No matter what he sets his mind to, he has the power to achieve it; he has proven that time and time again.

When asked how he deals with naysayers, Bryce answered, "I stay away from it. I stay with the people that I love. Every day, I get to do what I love, and that's what it's all about" (Abbate, 2019, paras. 13, 15).

Achievement Unlocked: Check Out Bryce Harper's Cool Career Awards!

Bryce's story teaches us an important lesson: To achieve your goals, you have to silence the noise and keep going, one step at a time. It's thanks to Bryce's laser focus and never-give-up attitude that he has earned a number of cool awards and achievements, including:

- **The Silver Slugger Award (2015, 2021, 2023):** This special award goes to the best hitter at each position in the National League. Bryce was recognized as the top slugger multiple times because of his amazing hitting skills. It proves that he's a force to be reckoned with at the plate!

- **1st All-MLB Team (2021):** Bryce was chosen for the All-MLB Team, a special award that celebrates the best players from all teams in Major League Baseball. Bryce earned this honor because fans and baseball experts agreed he was one of the very best outfielders that year. Are we surprised, though?

- **Player's Choice Outstanding Player of the Year Award (2021):** He wasn't just cheered on by fans and experts—his fellow athletes thought he was the absolute best that year too! This award, voted on by MLB players themselves, shows how much everyone admires Bryce for his amazing skills and cool attitude on the field.

- **N.L.C.S. Most Valuable Player Award (2022):** Bryce's standout performances in the National League Championship Series showed that he's truly at his best when the stakes are highest, and that's why he was named the MVP!

- **Hickok Belt (2022):** The Hickok Belt is given every year to the best professional athlete in the United States. Bryce was honored with this award in 2022 for his outstanding achievements and contributions to Major League Baseball. This further solidified his reputation as one of the most respected and influential players of his generation. In short, Bryce Harper is a pretty big deal, not just in baseball but in the entire sports world (*Bryce Harper Awards*, n.d.).

These are just a few of the many awards this baseball prodigy has earned; there are lots more out there. Bryce has also managed to set and break multiple records, almost year after year. For instance, in 2012, he received his first invite to play in an All-Star Game; at just 19 years old, he became the youngest position player—someone who plays both in the field and at bat—to participate in it. A few months later, he became the first teenager since 1964 to steal home plate, showing off his extraordinary speed. When Bryce hit his first career Major League home run, he became the youngest player to homer in the Major Leagues since 1998. By the way, these achievements all happened during his rookie year! And there were many more that followed.

Beyond the baseball field, Bryce actively contributes to making a positive impact through charity work and community involvement. For example, he has supported organizations like the Leukemia & Lymphoma Society, raising awareness and funds for cancer research. His efforts were recognized in 2018 when TIME magazine named him one of the 100 Most Influential People. Bryce used his dream of playing baseball professionally as a way to inspire others and make the world a better place.

"I'd rather be a good person off the field than a good baseball player on the field," Bryce once said, which is a pretty big deal because it shows that even though he's all about winning and achieving his goals, Bryce believes being kind is even more important (Harper, n.d.).

Did You Know?

Think you know everything about your favorite player, Bryce Harper? Here are some cool trivia to add to your list of fun facts:

- **Bryce is a… blind barber?** No, not literally! Blind Barber is just the name of the barbershop he's a part-owner of. It's a unique spot where you can get a fresh haircut and a refreshing drink right after. You might find it surprising that he owns a barbershop. That's because, as his popularity grew, so did the popularity of his luscious hair. At one point, there were actually 16 accounts dedicated specifically to his hair on the social media platform X, formerly known as Twitter (Bicks, 2024).
- **Bryce is huge fan of the Las Vegas Golden Knights hockey team:** You might catch him cheering from the stands at their games, showing his hometown pride and love for hockey!
- **Bryce's fans are known as "Harper's Heroes":** They're a dedicated bunch who love his playing style and charm so much that they coined the name themselves, and it just stuck (Minor, 2024).
- **Here's a rapid-fire list of some of Bryce's favorites:** His go-to cereal? Cheerios, but not Honey Nut—just the standard kind. Movie? It used to be *Titanic* until *Avatar* came along. Believe it or not, Bryce even has a favorite font. Spoiler alert: it's Courier! All great choices if you ask me (ESPN.com, 2010).

- **Bryce has a weird pre-game ritual:** Every game day has to go exactly the same way. He arrives at the field precisely at noon. He eats Eggo waffles. And he takes not one, not two, but seven showers before the first pitch. That's right—seven showers! He's definitely squeaky clean once he gets on the field (Yuscavage, 2013).

Chapter Activity: Shield of Strength

Bryce stayed strong and kept going, no matter what. To make sure he was focused on his goals, he shielded himself from negativity and bad influences. Now, it's your turn to create a special shield! Your shield could be anything that keeps you moving forward toward your dreams.

Ready? Here's how:

1. Think about what makes you feel strong and confident. It could be your friends, family, hobbies, favorite sports, or anything else that uplifts you.
2. Gather materials like a paper plate, markers, stickers, glitter, glue, and any other decorations you enjoy.
3. Use the paper plate as the base of your shield. Decorate it with all the things that inspire and motivate you.
4. Keep your shield in a place where you can see it every day.

Well done! Whenever you face challenges or negativity, look at your shield. Remind yourself that you are strong and that you can definitely overcome obstacles and achieve your goals. Rest, adjust your plans if needed, but always keep moving forward, no matter what, just like Bryce did!

What are some of the things you do to block out distractions and stay focused on your goals?

Inspire and Motivate!

All the greatest baseball players inspire others to become the best versions of themselves—and you can follow in their footsteps and spread the inspiration yourself.

Simply by sharing your honest opinion of this book and a little about the baseball heroes who have inspired you, you'll continue their work and motivate others to become the best version of themselves they can possibly be.

MAKE A LASTING IMPRESSION!

Thank you so much for your support. Use every challenge as an opportunity, and get out there and hit that home run!

Scan the QR code below

CONCLUSION

Awesome work! You've reached the last page! I hope you enjoyed reading about some of today's baseball legends and underdogs. Their stories aren't just about the sport—they're packed with important lessons to learn from. Just like in baseball, life is full of challenges and setbacks. But with perseverance, mental toughness, and teamwork, you can overcome any obstacle and achieve your dreams!

So, what's next? Take these stories to heart and apply what you've learned in your own life. To help you remember, think GLOVETALES:

- **G**rasp greatness regardless of your size, just as José Altuve did.
- **L**earn and practice to get better every day, just like Mookie Betts.
- **O**vercome obstacles by working together, as shown by Aaron Judge.

- **V**alue the people who believe in you, just as Clayton Kershaw does.
- **E**mbrace the idea of never giving up, just like Cody Bellinger.
- **T**ackle tough times with limitless determination, like Freddie Freeman.
- **A**lways find a way to bounce back from setbacks, just like Mike Trout.
- **L**ead by showing up every day, like Francisco Lindor.
- **E**ndure challenges by believing in yourself, just as Anthony Rizzo did.
- **S**tay strong and keep going, no matter what, like Bryce Harper.

By embracing these lessons and following the examples of these awesome athletes, you can face any challenge and come out stronger on the other side. Now, what are you waiting for? Go out there and hit life out of the park!

Did you find these stories inspiring? If so, consider leaving a review on Amazon. Your feedback helps others discover these tales and reminds them that they too can become great.

REFERENCES

Abbate, E. (2019, April 1). Bryce Harper on his pre-game training and why he stays off the internet. *Men's Health*. https://www.menshealth.com/fitness/a27003359/bryce-harper-training-diet/

Adler, D. (2021, May 17). *Yes, Kershaw can hold 6 baseballs in 1 hand*. MLB.com. https://www.mlb.com/news/clayton-kershaw-holds-six-baseballs-in-one-hand

AIM (Acts Inspired by Mookie). (n.d.). AIM Foundation. https://www.theaimfoundation.org/

Alipour, S. (2020, November 4). Dodgers' Cody Bellinger on world series win, lakers co-celebration and appearance in the new Assassin's Creed. *ESPN*. https://www.espn.ph/mlb/story/_/id/30251937/dodgers-cody-bellinger-world-series-win-lakers-co-celebration-appearance-new-assassin-creed

Anthony Rizzo awards. (n.d.). Baseball Almanac. https://www.baseball-almanac.com/players/awards

Anthony Rizzo was naked when he made his motivational speeches before Cubs' final 3 world series wins. (2017, March 14). *CBS Chicago*. https://www.cbsnews.com/chicago/news/anthony-rizzo-was-naked-when-he-made-his-motivational-speeches-before-cubs-final-3-world-series-wins/

Apstein, S. (2020, December 22). How Mookie Betts set The Dodgers on a championship path. *Sports Illustrated*. https://www.si.com/mlb/2020/12/22/mookie-betts-dodgers-world-series-sportsperson

Ardaya, F. (2022, May 1). Clayton Kershaw passes Don Sutton for Dodgers all-time strikeouts record. *The New York Times*. https://www.nytimes.com/athletic/4179155/2022/05/01/clayton-kershaw-passes-don-sutton-for-dodgers-all-time-strikeouts-record/

Bellinger, C. (n.d.). *30 best Cody Bellinger quotes with image*. Bookey. https://www.bookey.app/quote-author/cody-bellinger

Berg, T. (2014, July 15). 5 things you should know about Atlanta Braves All-Star Freddie Freeman. *For the Win*. https://ftw.usatoday.com/2014/07/freddie-freeman-atlanta-braves-all-star-mlb

Betts, M. (n.d.-a). *30 best Mookie Betts quotes with image*. Bookey. https://www.bookey.app/quote-author/mookie-betts

Betts, M. (n.d.-b). *Mookie Betts quotes*. FamousQuotes123. https://www.famousquotes123.com/mookie-betts-8807.html

Bicks, E. (2024, February 9). *Bryce harper: 5 fast facts you need to know*. Heavy. https://heavy.com/sports/2019/02/bryce-harper/

Bollinger, R. (2023, November 26). *Trout uses reach to make impact off the field*. MLB.com. https://www.mlb.com/news/mike-trout-put-spotlight-on-mental-health-awareness-in-2023

Bowman, M. (2017, March 16). *Freeman wholeheartedly endorses Classic experience*. MLB.com. https://www.mlb.com/news/freddie-freeman-on-wbc-2017-experience-c219443714

Brookover, B. (2019, April 1). *Bryce Harper's mythical journey from Las Vegas to Philadelphia, after seven turbulent seasons in D.C.* The Philadelphia Inquirer. https://www.inquirer.com/phillies/bryce-harper-life-story-las-vegas-nationals-phillies-future-20190401.html

Bryce Harper awards. (n.d.). Baseball Almanac. https://www.baseball-almanac.com/players/awards

Cassavell, A. (2015, January 28). *Rizzo's triumph over cancer takes stage on Network special*. MLB.com. https://www.mlb.com/news/anthony-rizzos-triumph-over-cancer-featured-on-mlb-network/c-107677800

Chu, D. (2023, July 28). Clayton Kershaw and his wife bring their four children to pitcher's charity ping pong tournament. *People*. https://people.com/clayton-kershaw-wife-four-kids-dodgers-charity-ping-pong-tournament-7567046

Clair, M. (2018, May 8). *Cody Bellinger appeared on Jimmy Kimmel and revealed the secret to his success is crepes*. MLB.com. https://www.mlb.com/cut4/cody-bellinger-appeared-on-jimmy-kimmel-c275781366

Clary, H. (2015, May 16). *Bryce harper and KrisBryanthave taken similar yet different paths to stardom*. Bleacher Report. https://bleacherreport.com/articles/2476108-bryce-harper-and-kris-bryant-have-taken-similar-yet-different-paths-to-stardom

Clayton Kershaw awards. (n.d.). Baseball Almanac. https://www.baseball-almanac.com/players/awards

Cody Bellinger biography & Los Angeles Dodgers career. (2020, March 19). Dodger Blue. https://dodgerblue.com/cody-bellinger-biography-los-angeles-dodgers-career-stats/

Colby, A. (2021, March 10). *Francisco Lindor ('11) donates toward new middle school building*. Montverde Academy. https://montverde.org/francisco-lindor-11-donates-toward-new-middle-school-building/

Colin. (2016, May 3). *Jose Altuve*. The MY HERO Project. https://myhero.com/J_Altuve_trhs_US_2016_ul

Crasnick, J. (2010, June 3). Yeah, he's that good. *ESPN*. https://www.espn.com/mlb/draft2010/columns/story?columnist=crasnick_jerry&id=5248377

Crasnick, J. (2012, May 16). Jose Altuve just keeps showing up. *ESPN*. https://www.espn.ph/mlb/story/_/id/7933839/houston-astros-their-very-own-little-engine-could

Dedaj, P. (2023, May 15). Dodgers pitcher Clayton Kershaw's mom dies day before Mother's Day. *Fox News*. https://www.foxnews.com/sports/dodgers-pitcher-clayton-kershaws-mom-dies-day-mothers-day

DiGiovanna, M. (2020, October 12). Braves star Freddie Freeman's formative years in Orange marked by tragedy and support. *Los Angeles Times*. https://www.latimes.com/sports/dodgers/story/2020-10-12/braves-freddie-freeman-orange-el-modena-mom-cancer-dad-support

Duarte, M. (2017, August 27). All of the Dodgers nicknames for Players Weekend explained. *NBC Los Angeles*. https://www.nbclosangeles.com/news/sports/all-of-the-dodgers-nicknames-for-players-weekend-explained/22754/

ESPN News Services. (2023, May 2). Bryce Harper rejoins Phillies 160 days after Tommy John surgery. *ESPN*. https://www.espn.com/mlb/story/_/id/37083257/phillies-activate-bryce-harper-160-days-tommy-john-surgery

ESPN.com. (2010, September 25). *These are some of bryceharper's favorite things*. https://www.espn.com/blog/sportscenter/post/_/id/82368/these-are-some-of-bryce-harper%E2%80%99s-favorite-things

Francisco Lindor. (n.d.). Stance. Retrieved July 19, 2024, from https://www.stance.com/the-thread/francisco-lindor-interview.html

Feinsand, M. (2024, June 6). *Here's how the Yanks landed Judge in '13 draft*. MLB.com. https://www.mlb.com/yankees/news/featured/oral-history-of-yankees-drafting-aaron-judge-c278026828

Fenno, N., & DiGiovanna, M. (2014, November 12). Great read: Angels' Mike Trout: from can't-miss kid to likely AL MVP in five years. *Los Angeles Times*. https://www.latimes.com/sports/la-sp-c1-angels-trout-20141112-story.html

Francisco Lindor awards. (n.d.). Baseball Almanac. https://www.baseball-almanac.com/players/awards

Freddie Freeman of the Atlanta Braves fights back for his mom. (2016, September 23). 3BL Media. https://www.3blmedia.com/news/freddie-freeman-atlanta-braves-fights-back-his-mom

Freeman, F. (n.d.-a). *30 best Freddie Freeman quotes with image.* Bookey. https://www.bookey.app/quote-author/freddie-freeman

Freeman, F. (n.d.-b). *Freddie Freeman quotes.* BrainyQuote. https://www.brainyquote.com/quotes/freddie_freeman_781941

Frommer, F. (2024). Bryce Harper. In *Encyclopaedia Britannica.* https://www.britannica.com/biography/Bryce-Harper

Garrity, T. (2023, June 26). Mookie Betts' hack for staying healthy on the road. *InsideHook.* https://www.insidehook.com/wellness/mookie-betts-routine-road-trips

Gonzalez, A. (2015a, April 18). *Trout goes deep; youngest to 100 HRs, 100 SBs.* MLB.com. https://www.mlb.com/news/angels-outfielder-mike-trout-smashes-100th-career-home-run/c-118949336

Gonzalez, A. (2015b, May 21). *Trout develops aptitude for hitting high pitches.* MLB.com. https://www.mlb.com/news/mike-trout-develops-aptitude-for-hitting-high-pitches/c-125835364

Gonzalez, A. (2015c, June 10). *Brother of Trout's girlfriend drafted by Angels.* MLB.com. https://www.mlb.com/angels/news/brother-of-mike-trouts-girlfriend-drafted-by-angels-in-mlb-draft/c-129799734

Grant, T. (2024). Aaron Judge. In *Encyclopedia Britannica.* https://www.britannica.com/biography/Aaron-Judge

Green, A. (2019, August 11). *Watch: Los Angeles Dodgers Foundation, Clayton Kershaw & Cody Bellinger Convince 9-Year-Old To Keep Playing Baseball As Part Of "Don't Retire, Kid" Campaign.* Dodger Blue. https://dodgerblue.com/watch-los-angeles-dodgers-foundation-clayton-kershaw-cody-bellinger-convince-9-year-old-keep-playing-baseball-dont-retire-kid-campaign/2019/08/11/

Hall, B. (2018, March 21). *How growing up "undersized" helped Cody Bellinger win MVP.* Stack. https://www.stack.com/a/once-a-lanky-teen-cody-bellinger-offers-crucial-advice-to-undersized-youth-athletes/

Harper, B. (n.d.-a). *Bryce Harper quotes.* A-Z Quotes. https://www.azquotes.com/author/6277-Bryce_Harper

Harper, B. (n.d.-b). *Bryce Harper quotes.* BrainyQuote. https://www.brainyquote.com/quotes/bryce_harper_520124

Harrigan, T. (2020, March 19). *9 times Clayton Kershaw made history.* MLB.com. https://www.mlb.com/news/clayton-kershaw-historic-career-moments

Harris, J. (2019, August 24). Dodgers' Cody Bellinger learned to love baseball at the Little League World Series. *Los Angeles Times*. https://www.latimes.com/sports/dodgers/story/2019-08-23/cody-bellinger-little-league-world-series-2007-clay-dodgers

Harris, J. (2023, April 14). Dodgers couldn't make Cody Bellinger a star again. "Sometimes you just don't have any answers." *Los Angeles Times*. https://www.latimes.com/sports/dodgers/story/2023-04-14/dodgers-cody-bellinger-dave-roberts-career-slide-chicago-cubs

Hispanic Heritage Month. (n.d.). *José Altuve*. https://www.hispanicheritage month.org/famous-hispanic-people/jose-altuve/

Huddleston, T. (2018, October 23). Dodgers star Mookie Betts was too small to make a Little League team—so his mom started her own. *CNBC*. https://www.cnbc.com/2018/10/23/how-boston-red-sox-mookie-betts-mom-became-his-first-baseball-coach.html

Jaffe, J. (2014, May 14). Human after all: A closer look into Mike Trout's May slump. *Sports Illustrated*. https://www.si.com/mlb/2014/05/14/mike-trout-slumping-los-angeles-angels

James, P. (2016, July 16). *Freeman has mole with cancerous cells removed*. MLB.com. https://www.mlb.com/news/braves-freddie-freeman-has-mole-removed-c189801388

Judge, A. (n.d.). *Aaron Judge quotes*. BrainyQuote. https://www.brainyquote.com/quotes/aaron_judge_948342

Kaneko, G. (2018, July 18). *It's time to become better acquainted with your new favorite superstar, Francisco Lindor*. MLB.com. https://www.mlb.com/cut4/five-facts-about-america-s-sweetheart-francisco-lindor-c286357830

Keown, T. (2016, March 10). Sorry not sorry. *ESPN*. https://www.espn.com/espn/feature/story/_/id/14935765/washington-nationals-bryce-harper-wants-change-baseball-forever

Kepner, T. (2021, November 4). The heart and soul of a franchise shines through. *The New York Times*. https://www.nytimes.com/2021/11/03/sports/baseball/freddie-freeman-braves-world-series.html

Kershaw, C. (n.d.). *30 best Clayton Kershaw quotes with image*. Bookey. https://www.bookey.app/quote-author/clayton-kershaw

Kershaw, C. (2019, June 13). Dad life. *The Players' Tribune*. https://www.theplayerstribune.com/articles/clayton-kershaw-fathers-day-dodgers

Kershaw's Challenge. (n.d.). *About*. Retrieved June 16, 2024, from https://www.kershawschallenge.com/about

Kiddle Encyclopedia. (2023). Aaron Judge facts for kids. In *Kiddle Encyclopedia*. https://kids.kiddle.co/Aaron_Judge

Kiddle Encyclopedia. (2024a). Anthony Rizzo facts for kids. In *Kiddle Encyclopedia*. https://kids.kiddle.co/Anthony_Rizzo

Kiddle Encyclopedia. (2024b). Bryce Harper facts for kids. In *Kiddle Encyclopedia*. https://kids.kiddle.co/Bryce_Harper

Kiddle Encyclopedia. (2024c). Cody Bellinger facts for kids. In *Kiddle Encyclopedia*. https://kids.kiddle.co/Cody_Bellinger

Kiddle Encyclopedia. (2024d). Freddie Freeman facts for kids. In *Kiddle Encyclopedia*. https://kids.kiddle.co/Freddie_Freeman

Kiddle Encyclopedia. (2024e). Mike Trout facts for kids. In *Kiddle Encyclopedia*. https://kids.kiddle.co/Mike_Trout

Kilgore, A. (n.d.). Bryce Harper: A swing of beauty. *The Washington Post*. https://www.washingtonpost.com/wp-srv/special/sports/bryce-harper-swing-of-beauty/

Kuty, B. (2018, July 27). *Yankees' Aaron Judge breaks wrist | What it means*. NJ.com. https://www.nj.com/yankees/2018/07/yankees_aaron_judge_out_at_least_3_weeks_what_it_m.html

Kyle, B. (2021, October 31). *The improbable journey of Houston Astros' Jose Altuve: From Venezuela sandlot to world champion*. Front Row & Backstage. https://bradkyle.substack.com/p/the-improbable-journey-of-houston

Ladson, B. (2023, August 15). *Lindor delivers Mets' first 20-20 season in 15 years*. MLB.com. https://www.mlb.com/news/francisco-lindor-reaches-20-20-season-in-mets-win

Lindor, F. (2019, April 19). Back to baseball. *The Players' Tribune*. https://www.theplayerstribune.com/articles/francisco-lindor-cleveland-indians

Lord, A. (2023, August 1). *Freddie Freeman shares hilarious Braves minor league story*. SportsTalkATL. https://www.sportstalkatl.com/freddie-freeman-shares-hilarious-braves-minor-league-story/

Maciborski, N. (2019, April 26). *Yankees magazine: Something more to give*. MLB.com. https://www.mlb.com/news/aaron-judge-is-a-true-leader

Magruder, J. (2018, May 6). *Altuve collecting baseball gear for Venezuela*. MLB.com. https://www.mlb.com/news/jose-altuve-donating-gloves-to-venezuela-c275443130

Masih, A. (2022, December 29). *When Yankees superstar Aaron Judge spoke about maintaining a fine balance between three sports in high school*. Sprortskeeda. https://www.sportskeeda.com/baseball/when-yankees-superstar-aaron-judge-spoke-maintaining-fine-balance-three-sports-high-school

McCaffrey, J. (2015a, April 30). *Watch Mookie Betts complete a Rubik's Cube in 1:52 seconds*. Masslive. https://www.masslive.com/redsox/2015/04/boston_red_sox_center_fielder_2.html

McCaffrey, J. (2015b, July 16). What's Mookie Betts' real name? How Markus became Mookie. *Mass Live Media*. https://www.masslive.com/redsox/2015/07/what_is_mookie_betts_real_name.html

McCormick, M. (2017, August 27). *Rizzos are Little League Parents of the Year*. MLB.com. https://www.mlb.com/news/anthony-rizzo-s-parents-feted-by-little-league-c250762830

McCullough, A. (2017, May 13). Cody Bellinger, Dodgers' latest can't-miss kid, has been right on the mark. *Los Angeles Times*. https://www.latimes.com/sports/dodgers/la-sp-dodgers-bellinger-20170513-story.html

McCullough, A. (2024, May 8). How Clayton Kershaw made the senior year leap. *D Magazine*. https://www.dmagazine.com/sports/2024/05/clayton-kershaw-book-excerpt/

McTaggart, B. (2014, May 6). *Altuve proud to draw praise from Vizquel*. MLB.com. https://www.mlb.com/news/altuve-proud-to-draw-praise-from-vizquel/c-74543336

Meisel, Z. (2015, March 3). Cleveland Indians top prospect Francisco Lindor is ignoring the hype: "I don't want to be God." *Cleveland.com*. https://www.cleveland.com/tribe/2015/03/cleveland_indians_francisco_li.html

Mercury News. (2016, August 12). Bryce Harper: A swing of beauty. *The Mercury News*. https://www.mercurynews.com/2013/05/12/bryce-harper-a-swing-of-beauty/

Miller, R. (2021, October 18). *Getting to know Yankees' Anthony Rizzo, a cancer survivor who embraces N.J. roots and passed on COVID vaccine*. NJ.com. https://www.nj.com/yankees/2021/07/getting-to-know-yankees-anthony-rizzo-a-cancer-survivor-who-embraces-nj-roots-and-passed-on-covid-vaccine.html

Miller, S. (2016, June 9). How prep phenom Clayton Kershaw became an L.A. Dodger 10 years ago. *Bleacher Report*. https://bleacherreport.com/articles/2642794-how-prep-phenom-clayton-kershaw-became-an-la-dodger-10-years-ago

Minor, A. (2024, May 30). *17 fascinating facts about Bryce Harper*. Facts.net. https://facts.net/celebrity/17-fascinating-facts-about-bryce-harper/

Monagan, M. (2020, November 21). *Belli's toe tap is the hip new HR celebration*.

MLB.com. https://www.mlb.com/news/cody-bellinger-foot-tap-celebration

Mookie and Brianna Betts' 50/50 Foundation makes donation to UCLA Mattel Children's Hospital. (n.d.). 5050 Foundation. https://www.the5050foundation.org/post/mookie-and-brianna-betts-50-50-foundation-makes-donation-to-ucla-mattel-children-s-hospital

Moshier, R. (2013, July 21). All-MV Baseball Player of the Year: Anthony Rizzo. *Utica Observer Dispatch.* https://www.uticaod.com/story/news/education/graduation/2013/07/21/all-mv-baseball-player-year/41627752007/

Mustard, E. (2015, July 15). Did you know Clayton Kershaw's great uncle discovered Pluto? *Sports Illustrated.* https://www.si.com/extra-mustard/2015/07/15/pluto-dodgers-clayton-kershaw-uncle-clyde-tombaugh

Nathan, A. (2017, June 21). *Cody Bellinger becomes 1st rookie to hit 10 home runs in 10 games.* Bleacher Report. https://bleacherreport.com/articles/2716917-cody-bellinger-becomes-1st-rookie-to-hit-10-home-runs-in-10-games

Neumann, S. (2023, May 15). Mom of Dodgers Pitcher Clayton Kershaw dies the day before Mother's Day: "He has a heavy heart." *People.* https://people.com/sports/mother-of-dodgers-pitcher-clayton-kershaw-dies/

New York Yankees First Baseman Anthony Rizzo Teams Up with CHAMpions for CHAM Runners to Support Patients and Their Families | Update. (2023, August 2). Montefiore Einstein. https://montefioreeinsteinnow.org/update/2023-aug-2/anthony-rizzo-champions-for-cham

Nightengale, B. (2023, August 27). Nightengale's Notebook: Cody Bellinger's revival with Cubs has ex-MVP primed for big payday. *USA Today.* https://www.usatoday.com/story/sports/mlb/columnist/bob-nightengale/2023/08/27/cody-bellinger-chicago-cubs-nl-wild-card-free-agent/70694462007/

O'Connell, R. (2020, May 27). *Jose Altuve: 5 fast facts you need to know.* Heavy. https://heavy.com/sports/2017/07/jose-altuve-jump-swing-all-star-astros/

O'Shea, T. (2023, October 20). Bryce Harper: The untold story of His JUCO struggles. *Joker Mag.* https://jokermag.com/bryce-harper-juco-story/

Olney, B. (2018, August 1). Inside the discovery of Mike Trout. *ABC7.* https://abc7.com/3843006/

Osborne, C. (2022, August 20). *Freeman pays his high school back by paying it forward.* Medium. https://dodgers.mlblogs.com/freeman-pays-his-high-school-back-by-paying-it-forward-2c6ab095e74e

Parrales, J. (2020, July 24). *5 key facts to know about Mookie Betts*. Pro Sports Outlook. https://prosportsoutlook.com/5-key-facts-to-know-about-mookie-betts/

Pasillas, C. (2023, April 15). *Dodgers news: Cody Bellinger thought he'd be in LA for life*. Dodgers Nation. https://dodgersnation.com/dodgers-news-cody-bellinger-thought-hed-be-in-la-for-life/2023/04/15/

Piellucci, M. (2023, April 12). Faith, family, and fastballs: Clayton Kershaw has always belonged to Dallas. *D Magazine*. https://www.dmagazine.com/publications/d-magazine/2023/april/clayton-kershaw-faith-family-and-fastballs/

Pisano, M. (2016, November 8). 20 facts you should know about Anthony Rizzo. *Emme Magazine*. https://www.emme-magazine.com/2016/11/08/anthonyrizzo/

Players working to overcome language barrier. (2013, March 4). MLB.com. https://www.mlb.com/news/italian-players-in-world-baseball-classic-working-to-overcome-language-barrier/c-42260910

Pleskoff, B. (2022, January 18). Re-signing Freddie Freeman should be Braves' top priority, but here are three other options at first. *Forbes*. https://www.forbes.com/sites/berniepleskoff/2022/01/18/signing-first-baseman-freddie-freeman-should-be-a-priority-for-the-atlanta-braves/

Pleskoff, B. (2023, November 3). *The unique story behind Jose Altuve signing with the Houston Astros*. Forbes. https://www.forbes.com/sites/berniepleskoff/2023/11/03/the-unique-story-behind-jose-altuve-signing-with-the-houston-astros/?sh=5aa0bba02963

Puma, Mi. (2021, January 7). Five things Mets fans may not know about Francisco Lindor. *New York Post*. https://nypost.com/2021/01/07/five-things-mets-fans-may-not-know-about-francisco-lindor/

Randhawa, M. (2024, June 16). *Like father, like son -- these players shared their dad's number*. MLB.com. https://www.mlb.com/news/mlb-fathers-sons-with-same-number

What charitable causes benefit from Jose Altuve's baseball success? (2023, June 12). RevUp Sports. https://revupsports.com/athletes/baseball/jose-altuve/discover/jose-altuve-charity-contributions/

Reynoso, J. (2023, July 31). Dodgers news: Mookie Betts didn't want to be traded to LA in 2020. *FanNation*. https://www.si.com/mlb/dodgers/news/dodgers-news-mookie-betts-didnt-want-to-be-traded-to-la-in-2020-jr2003

Rizzo, A. (n.d.-a). *A note from Anthony.* Anthony Rizzo Family Foundation. https://arizzofoundation.org/about

Rizzo, A. (n.d.-b). *Anthony Rizzo quotes.* BrainyQuote. https://www.brainyquote.com/authors/anthony-rizzo-quotes

Rogers, J. (2023, August 23). How 2019 MVP Cody Bellinger revived his career with Cubs. *ESPN.com.* https://www.espn.ph/mlb/story/_/id/38233363/cody-bellinger-former-mvp-career-revived-chicago-cubs-dodgers

RotoWire Staff. (2024, March 13). Yankees' Aaron Judge: Battling oblique issue. *CBS Sports.* https://www.cbssports.com/fantasy/baseball/news/yankees-aaron-judge-battling-oblique-issue/

Sanchez, R. (2016, September 28). When Anthony Rizzo was diagnosed with cancer, Jon Lester threw him a lifeline. *ESPN.com.* https://www.espn.com/mlb/story/_/id/17659023/cancer-survivors-contenders-anthony-rizzo-jon-lester-bond-goes-deeper-cubs

Sandler, T. (2020a, August 5). 5 fun facts about Aaron Judge. *Fangirl Sports Network.* https://fgsn.com/5-fun-facts-about-aaron-judge/

Sandler, T. (2020b, September 2). *5 fun facts about Mookie Betts.* Fangirl Sports Network. https://fgsn.com/5-fun-facts-about-mookie-betts

Sandler, T. (2021, March 31). 5 fun facts about Clayton Kershaw. *Fangirl Sports Network.* https://fgsn.com/5-fun-facts-about-clayton-kershaw/

Sandler, T. (2022a, April 6). 5 fun facts about Mike Trout. *Fangirl Sports Network.* https://fgsn.com/5-fun-facts-about-mike-trout/

Sandler, T. (2022b, May 11). *5 fun facts about Anthony Rizzo.* Fangirl Sports Network. https://fgsn.com/5-fun-facts-about-anthony-rizzo/

Santasiere III, A. (2024, May 17). *Yankees Mag: The good in mankind.* MLB.com. https://www.mlb.com/news/yankees-magazine-anthony-rizzo-s-charity-work

Schreffler, L. (2023, March 8). Francisco Lindor sleeps easily every night — clad in designer watches. *Haute Living.* https://hauteliving.com/2023/03/francisco-lindor-haute-living-cover-story/

Schube, S. (2021, March 16). Mookie Betts can't stop getting better. *GQ.* https://www.gq.com/story/dodgers-mookie-betts-profile

Scipioni, J. (2021, April 1). World Series champ Cody Bellinger on "little mental gimmicks" that help him mentally prepare for a game. *CNBC.* https://www.cnbc.com/2021/04/01/how-mlb-star-cody-bellinger-mentally-prepares-for-a-game-.html

Selbe, N. (2022, October 9). Dodgers' Mookie Betts gets perfect 300 game in bowling. *Sports Illustrated*. https://www.si.com/extra-mustard/2022/10/09/dodgers-mookie-betts-bowls-perfect-300-game

Serby, S. (2023, April 16). Francisco Lindor on Mets success, family adversity, Buck Showalter. *New York Post*. https://nypost.com/2023/04/15/francisco-lindor-on-mets-success-family-adversity-buck-showalter/

Sheinin, D. (2011, March 13). For the love of Bryce Harper. *Washington Post*. https://www.washingtonpost.com/lifestyle/magazine/for-the-love-of-bryce-harper/2011/01/17/ABbi9SP_story.html

Shelburne, R. (2010, July 11). Angels' Trout a diamond in the rough. *ESPN*. https://www.espn.com/los-angeles/mlb/news/story?id=5371199

Shiffer, Emily J., and Joshua St. Clair. *The 35 Best Baseball Quotes of All Time*. Men's Health. Last modified April 13, 2021. https://www.menshealth.com/entertainment/a33792852/baseball-quotes/

Smith, B. (2013, April 1). Can Anthony Rizzo break the cubs curse? *Chicago Magazine*. https://www.chicagomag.com/chicago-magazine/may-2013/anthony-rizzo/

Stevens, P. (2023, September 9). Freddie Freeman hits 53rd double of season, setting Dodgers record. *CBC News*. https://www.cbc.ca/sports/baseball/mlb/freddie-freeman-dodgers-record-53-doubles-mlb-1.6961882

Thosar, D. (2024, May 20). How Aaron Judge broke out of the biggest slump of his career: "There's no panic in him." *FOX Sports*. https://www.foxsports.com/stories/mlb/how-aaron-judge-broke-out-of-the-biggest-slump-of-his-career-theres-no-panic-in-him

Togerson, D. (2011, June 9). *Rizzo's debut is wildly successful*. NBC 7 San Diego. https://www.nbcsandiego.com/news/local/rizzos-debut-is-wildly-successful/1899645/

Toribio, J. (2022, July 19). *Cooperstown the ultimate goal for hyper-driven Mookie*. MLB.com. https://www.mlb.com/news/mookie-betts-has-heart-set-on-hall-of-fame-career

Trezza, J. (2017, August 28). *LLWS was invaluable experience for Bellinger*. MLB.com. https://www.mlb.com/news/cody-bellinger-cherishes-llws-experience-c250929164

Trout, M. (n.d.). *Mike Trout quotes*. AZ Quotes. https://www.azquotes.com/quote/1597237

Verducci, T. (2009, June 8). Baseball's LeBron. *Sports Illustrated*. https://vault.si.com/vault/2009/06/08/baseballs-lebron

Villas, R. (2023, May 17). *Dodgers' Clayton Kershaw shares heartfelt message after first start since mother's death*. ClutchPoints. https://clutchpoints.

com/dodgers-news-clayton-kershaw-shares-heartfelt-message-after-first-start-since-mothers-death

Wagner, J. (2021, October 17). Freddie Freeman thinks you're doing a great job. *The New York Times*. https://www.nytimes.com/2021/10/07/sports/baseball/freddie-freeman-atlanta.html

Waldstein, D. (2019, October 21). The "aura of Altuve" powers the Astros. *The New York Times*. https://www.nytimes.com/2019/10/21/sports/baseball/jose-altuve-astros.html

Warren, S. (2022, October 6). America's new home-run king follows the king of kings: The remarkable story of Aaron Judge. *CBN*. https://www2.cbn.com/news/entertainment/americas-new-home-run-king-follows-king-kings-remarkable-story-aaron-judge

Wilson, J. (2023, October 13). Here's what Bryce Harper said about his injury after NLDS victory. *FanSided*. https://fansided.com/posts/here-s-what-bryce-harper-said-about-his-injury-after-nlds-victory-01hckhcqpnnz

Yancelson, B. (2015, July 9). Jose Altuve and the Astros are winning — and having fun while they're at it. *Sports Illustrated Kids*. https://www.sikids.com/kid-reporter/jose-altuve-has-astros-winning

Yazzie, K. (2024, May 30). *14 astonishing facts about Mike Trout*. Facts.net. https://facts.net/celebrity/14-astonishing-facts-about-mike-trout/

Yuscavage, C. (2013, January 17). Bryce harper has one of the weirdest pregame rituals ever. *Complex*. https://www.complex.com/sports/a/chris-yuscavage/bryce-harper-has-one-of-the-weirdest-pregame-rituals-ever

Made in United States
Orlando, FL
18 December 2024